Thai

An Essential Grammar

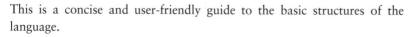

This is a concise and user-friendly guide to the basic structures of the language.

Grammatical forms are demonstrated through examples, given in both Thai script and romanised transliteration, with clear, jargon-free explanations. It is designed for use both by students taking a taught course in Thai and for independent learners, and includes guidance on pronunciation, speech conventions and the Thai writing system as well as grammar.

Topics include:

- Sentence particles
- Negation
- Questions
- Numerals and quantification
- Location markers and prepositions

With numerous examples bringing grammar to life, this unique reference work will prove invaluable to all students looking to master the grammar of Thai.

David Smyth is Lecturer in Thai at the School of Oriental and African Studies, University of London.

Routledge Essential Grammars

The following titles are available in the *Essential Grammars* series:

Chinese
Danish
Dutch
English
Finnish
Georgian: A Learner's Grammar
Hungarian
Modern Hebrew
Norwegian
Polish
Portuguese
Swedish
Urdu

Other titles of related interest published by Routledge:

Colloquial Thai
By John Moore and Saowalak Rodchue

Thai

An Essential Grammar

 **David Smyth**

 Routledge
Taylor & Francis Group

LONDON AND NEW YORK

First published 2002
by Routledge
11 New Fetter Lane, London EC4P 4EE

Simultaneously published in the USA and Canada
by Routledge
29 West 35th Street, New York, NY 10001

Reprinted 2004 (twice)

Routledge is an imprint of the Taylor & Francis Group

Typeset in Sabon and Gill
by Florence Production Ltd, Stoodleigh, Devon

Printed and bound in Great Britain
by TJ International Ltd, Padstow, Cornwall

British Library Cataloguing in Publication Data
A catalogue record for this book is available from the British Library.

Library of Congress Cataloging-in-Publication Data
A catalog record for this book has been requested

ISBN 0–415–22614–7 (pbk)
ISBN 0–415–22613–9 (hbk)

For Manas Chitakasem

Contents

Contents

Contents

Preface

This volume aims to fill a long-felt need, among both teachers and students of Thai, for a detailed descriptive grammar which is accessible to the ordinary learner with little or no knowledge of linguistic terminology. For beginners, it should prove a useful reference source that may be used in conjunction with any introductory language course; for more advanced learners, it will hopefully clarify grey areas in their knowledge and provide some further insight into the language.

This book could not have been attempted, let alone completed, without the help and encouragement of many people, over a period of many years. I am indebted to all those Thais who, over the years, with charm, grace and tact have helped me to improve my knowledge of their language; to all those authors listed in the bibliography (and many others, too numerous to mention); to the late Peter J. Bee, formerly Lecturer in Tai at the School of Oriental and African Studies, University of London, who did much to arouse my curiosity about language in general and Thai in particular; and to those students of Thai who each year ask new and searching questions and fill me with fresh resolve not to have to bluff my way through the following year. I am especially grateful to Sujinda Khantayalongkoch, Manas Chitakasem, Vantana Cornwell and Routledge's anonymous reviewer from Australia, for their careful checking of the draft manuscript and their numerous constructive suggestions for improving the text; their input has been invaluable. I am also grateful to Walaiporn Tantikanangkul, Andrew Simpson and Justin Watkins for some very practical guidance. Errors, omissions and other shortcomings that may remain are, however, entirely my own responsibility. Finally, my greatest debt of gratitude is to Manas Chitakasem, my teacher, colleague and friend for nearly thirty years, for his unstinting support and encouragement since my first faltering forays into Thai; it is to him that this book is dedicated with respect and affection.

Introduction

Thai and its speakers

Thai (formerly called 'Siamese') is a member of the *Tai* family of languages which are spoken by an estimated 70 million people dispersed over a wide area of Asia, from northern Vietnam to northern India. Thai, with nearly 50 million first-language speakers, is the most important language in the Tai family, which also includes Lao, Shan (spoken in northern Burma) and some 15 million speakers in southwestern China. Despite common structural features, even closely related Tai languages are often mutually unintelligible because of phonological and lexical differences. Tai speakers were once thought to have originated from China and migrated southwards, but today the border area between northern Vietnam and China's Guangxi province is regarded as a more likely origin. From the eighth century AD Tai speakers began to migrate westwards and south-westwards into what is present-day Thailand.

Thai is the national language of Thailand. Distinct regional dialects of Thai are spoken in the north, northeast and south of the country, but the language of the Central Region is regarded as the standard and is used both in schools and for official purposes throughout the country.

Thai is a tonal language, with the meaning of each syllable determined by the pitch at which it is pronounced. Standard Thai has five tones – mid, low, high, rising and falling. Thai has no noun or verb inflections: a noun has a single form, with no distinction between singular and plural, while past, present and future time can be conveyed by a single verb form. Like many other South-East Asian languages, Thai has a complex pronoun system, which reflects gender, age, social status, the formality of the situation and the degree of intimacy between speakers. Much of the original Thai lexicon is monosyllabic; a high percentage of polysyl-labic words are foreign borrowings, particularly from the classical Indian languages, Sanskrit and Pali.

Romanisation

There is no universally recognised system for romanising Thai and Thais can neither write their language in the Western alphabet nor easily read Westerners' romanisations of Thai. When romanising Thai, linguists use one system, librarians another and the Royal Thai Institute yet another; the average Thai, if called upon to romanise Thai words, would almost certainly do so in a quite unsystematic way.

The system used in this book is based on the phonemic transcription devised by the American scholar, Mary Haas, in the early 1940s and slightly modified in J. Marvin Brown's AUA Thai course materials. While this system is widely used in the linguistic literature on Thai and academic writing on Thailand, commercially published courses often avoid transcriptions that use symbols from the International Phonetic Alphabet. The system appears in full in Appendix 1.

Learning Thai

A number of readily available Thai courses can be used in conjunction with this grammar. The *Linguaphone Thai Course* (1984) by Manas Chitakasem and David Smyth, and *Teach Yourself Thai* (1995) by David Smyth, both equip the learner with the necessary grammar and vocabulary to deal with a range of everyday situations and provide a structured introduction to the script; both works include cassettes/CDs.

Of earlier materials, *Spoken Thai* (1945–8) by Mary Haas and Heng Subhanka, although dated in places, is an extremely solid work, which offers many valuable insights into the language. *Foundations of Thai* (1968) by Edward Anthony *et al.*, and *Thai Basic Course* (1970) by Warren G. Yates and Absorn Tryon likewise provide very thorough introductions to the language with comprehensive grammar notes. The *AUA Language Center Thai Course* (1967), prepared by J. Marvin Brown, is designed for classroom use with a native speaker, rather than self-tuition, but other works produced by AUA, including Brown's *AUA Language Center Thai Course: Reading and Writing* (1979), and Adrian Palmer's imaginative dialogue books, *Small Talk* (1974) and *Getting Help with Your Thai* (1977) are well worth consulting. *Fundamentals of the Thai Language* (1957) by Stuart Campbell and Chuan Shaweewongse (although in the most recent reprint, authorship is now attributed to 'the editors of Marketing Media Associates Co., Ltd.'), has long provided the Bangkok expatriate with a sound introduction to the language, despite its traditional grammar-translation approach.

Two substantial books on Thai grammar addressed to English speakers are *Thai Reference Grammar* (1964) by Richard Noss and *Teaching of Thai Grammar* (1982) by William Kuo. Noss's book, based on his doctoral thesis, is a detailed and insightful descriptive grammar that no serious student of Thai can fail to benefit from; however, it is addressed to those with a background in linguistics, and its use of linguistic terminology is at best bewildering and at times simply intimidating for the majority of beginners. Kuo's book, by contrast, is a much more down-to-earth workbook for practising key structures, but it does require a prior knowledge of Thai script.

Dictionaries

The most useful dictionary for the learner is *Thai-English Student's Dictionary* (1964) compiled by Mary Haas. Each Thai script entry is followed by a phonemic transcription and English gloss. A particularly useful feature for the learner is that for every noun the appropriate classifier is indicated; many of the entries also include well-chosen examples of everyday usage. George B. McFarland's *Thai-English Dictionary* (1944), although dated, remains a valuable reference work for the more advanced student of Thai, for it contains many words of Sanskrit origin and extensive listings of flora and fauna not found in the Haas volume. Two impressive recent works, which do not include pronunciation guides, but do reflect more up-to-date usage, are Domnern and Sathienpong's *Thai-English Dictionary* (1994) and Thianchai Iamwaramet's *A New Thai Dictionary with Bilingual Explanation* (1993). Robertson's *Practical English-Thai Dictionary* (1969) is an invaluable pocket-sized aid for the beginner, which gives Thai equivalents of about 2,500 common English words in both romanised transcription and Thai script.

Linguistic literature on Thai

There is a rich English-language literature on many aspects of Thai linguistics, most of which is catalogued in Franklin E. Huffman's *Bibliography and Index of Mainland Southeast Asian Languages and Linguistics* (1986). Much of this literature is in the form of unpublished doctoral theses written in American university linguistics departments during the 1970s and 1980s and therefore not readily available. A number of collections of essays produced to honour leading scholars of Thai, most notably William J. Gedney (1975), Fang-Kuei Li (1976) and Vichin Panupong (1997), include contributions which the serious learner can benefit from. Anthony Diller's essays on levels of language use (1985) and the role of Central Thai as a national language (1991) and William A. Smalley's *Linguistic Diversity and National Unity: Language Ecology in Thailand* (1994), a masterful study of the relationship between the national language, regional dialects and minority languages, are accessible to the layman and offer invaluable insights into the language and language situation in Thailand.

Chapter 1

Pronunciation

Thai differs radically from English and other European languages in being a *tone language*. In tone languages the meaning of a syllable is determined by the pitch at which it is pronounced. The Thai sound system also includes a small number of consonant and vowel sounds which have no close equivalent in English. The lists of consonant and vowel sounds in this section include, where possible, a close equivalent sound in standard British English. An example of the sound in a word is given for confirmation with a Thai native speaker.

1.1 Consonants

1.1.1 Initial consonants

The consonants **d, b, f, l, m, n, r, y, w, s, h** are similar to English; the following consonants, however, need further clarification:

k similar to *g* in *get* e.g. **kày** (ไก่) chicken

kh similar to *kh* in *khakhi* e.g. **khày** (ไข่) egg

ŋ similar to *ng* in *singer* e.g. **ŋaan** (งาน) work

c similar to *j* in *jar* e.g. **caan** (จาน) plate

ch similar to *ch* in *chart* e.g. **chaay** (ชาย) male

t similar to *t* in *stop* e.g. **taam** (ตาม) to follow

th similar to *th* in *Thailand* e.g. **thay** (ไทย) Thai

p similar to *p* in *spin* e.g. **pay** (ไป) to go

ph similar to *p* in *part* e.g. **phaasǎa** (ภาษา) language

5

Many Thais find it difficult to produce an initial **r** and will substitute **l**. Thus **rúu** ('to know') is often pronounced **lúu**.

| 1.1.2 | **Final consonants** |

A Thai syllable can end in two types of consonant sounds:

(a)   the stops **-p, -t, -k**

The final stop consonants are *unreleased*. Unreleased stops are produced when the airstream is closed to make the sound, but not re-opened, so that no air is released. Examples in English include the 'p' in the casual pronunciation of 'yep!' and the 't' in 'rat' when 'rat trap' is said quickly. Beginners sometimes find it difficult to hear the difference between words like **rák** ('to love'), **rát** ('to bind') and **ráp** ('to receive'), while in attempting to reproduce these sounds, they may inadvertently 'release' the final consonant.

(b)   the nasals **-m, -n, -ŋ**

These sounds are familiar from English and present no problem.

| 1.1.3 | **Consonant clusters** |

The following consonant clusters exist in Thai; they occur only at the beginning of a word:

kr- as in **kruŋ** (กรุง) city

kl- as in **klay** (ไกล) far

kw- as in **kwâaŋ** (กว้าง) wide

khr- as in **khray** (ใคร) who?

khl- as in **khláay** (คล้าย) to resemble

khw- as in **khwǎa** (ขวา) right

pr- as in **pratuu** (ประตู) door

pl- as in **plaa** (ปลา) fish

phr- as in **phrá** (พระ) monk

phl- as in **phlâat** (พลาด) to miss, fail

tr- as in **troŋ** (ตรง) straight

In everyday speech many Thais will omit the second consonant in a cluster:

plaa (ปลา) 'fish' becomes **paa**

khray (ใคร) 'who?' becomes **khay**

pratuu (ประตู) 'door' becomes **patuu**

A more radical transformation, associated with Bangkok working-class speech, is the change of initial **khw-** to **f-**:

khwǎa (ขวา) 'right' becomes **fǎa**

khwaam sùk (ความสุข) 'happiness' becomes **faam sùk**

1.2 Vowels and diphthongs

Thai distinguishes between short and long vowels. Short vowels are transcribed with a single letter (e.g. **-a**, **-e**, **-ə**, etc.) and long vowels with two letters (e.g. **-aa**, **-ee**, **-ii**, etc.).

Diphthongs (combinations of two vowel sounds) are similarly distinguished by length. Short diphthongs are represented by a single letter followed by **w** or **y** (e.g. **-aw**, **-ɔy**, **-uy**, etc.); long diphthongs are represented by either two different letters (e.g. **-ia**, **-ɯa**, **-ua**, etc.) or two similar letters followed by **w** or **y** (e.g **-aaw**, **-ɛɛw**, **- əəy**, etc.).

Learners are likely to experience some difficulty in hearing and producing differences between the short and long diphthongs **-aw/-aaw** and **-ay/-aay**:

raw	(เรา)	we	**raaw**	(ราว)	about
khâw	(เข้า)	to enter	**khâaw**	(ข้าว)	rice
tay	(ไต)	liver	**taay**	(ตาย)	to die
sǎy	(ใส)	clear	**sǎay**	(สาย)	late morning

When reading Thai script it is essential to be able to distinguish between long and short vowel symbols, as vowel length influences tone (see Chapter 2):

-a   similar to *u* in *run* e.g. **yaŋ** (ยัง) still

-aa   similar to *a* in *father* e.g. **maa** (มา) to come

-e   similar to *e* in *let* e.g. **dèk** (เด็ก) child

7

-ee	similar to *ay* in *may* e.g. **thee** (เท) to pour
-ə	similar to *er* in *number* e.g. **ŋən** (เงิน) money
-əə	similar to *er* in *her* e.g. **cəə** (เจอ) to meet
-ɛ	short vowel, similar to *air* in *hair* e.g. **khɛ̌ŋ** (แข็ง) hard
-ɛɛ	long vowel, similar to *air* in *hair* e.g. **mɛ̂ɛ** (แม่) mother
-i	similar to *i* in *bin* e.g. **bin** (บิน) to fly
-ii	similar to *ee* in *fee* e.g. **mii** (มี) to have
-ɔ	short vowel, similar to *or* in *corn* e.g. **tɔ̂ŋ** (ต้อง) must
-ɔɔ	long vowel, similar to *or* in *corn* e.g. **bɔ̀ɔk** (บอก) to say
-o	similar to *o* in *Ron* e.g. **con** (จน) poor
-oo	similar to *o* in *go* e.g. **too** (โต) big
-u	similar to *oo* in *book* e.g. **yúk** (ยุค) era
-uu	similar to *oo* in *coo* e.g. **rúu** (รู้) to know
-ʉ	short vowel, with no equivalent in English; e.g. **nʉ̀ŋ** (หนึ่ง) one
-ʉʉ	long vowel, with no equivalent in English; e.g. **mʉʉ** (มือ) hand
-ia	similar to *ear* in *hear* e.g. **sǐa** (เสีย) to lose
-ua	similar to *oer* in *doer* e.g. **rúa** (รั้ว) fence
-ʉa	long diphthong with no equivalent in English; e.g. **bʉ̀a** (เบื่อ) bored
-iaw	similar to *io* in *Rio* e.g. **diaw** (เดียว) single
-uay	similar to *oué* in *roué* e.g. **ruay** (รวย) rich
-ʉay	diphthong with no equivalent in English; e.g. **nʉ̀ay** (เหนื่อย) tired
-uy	similar to *ewy* in *chewy* e.g. **khuy** (คุย) to chat
-ooy	long diphthong with no equivalent in English; e.g. **dooy** (โดย) by
-əəy	long diphthong with no equivalent in English; e.g. **nəəy** (เนย) butter
-ɔy	similar to *oy* in *boy* e.g. **bɔ̀y** (บ่อย) often
-ɔɔy	similar to *oy* in *boy* e.g. **rɔ́ɔy** (ร้อย) hundred
-ay	short diphthong, similar to *ai* in *Thai* e.g. **thay** (ไทย) Thai

-aay	long diphthong, similar to *ai* in *Thai* e.g. **taay** (ตาย) dead
-iw	similar to *ue* in *hue* e.g. **hǐw** (หิว) hungry
-ew	short diphthong, similar to *ayo* in *Mayo* e.g. **rew** (เร็ว) fast
-eew	long diphthong, similar to *ayo* in *Mayo* e.g. **leew** (เลว) bad
-ɛw	short diphthong with no equivalent in English; e.g. **thɛ̌w** (แถว) row
-ɛɛw	long diphthong with no equivalent in English; e.g. **lɛ́ɛw** (แล้ว) already
-aw	short diphthong, similar to *ao* in *Lao* e.g. **raw** (เรา) we
-aaw	long diphthong, similar to *ao* in *Lao* e.g. **raaw** (ราว) about

1.3 Tones

Each syllable in Thai is pronounced with a specific tone. Standard Thai has five different tones, which are represented in the transcription system by an accent over the first vowel in the syllable. They are mid tone (no accent), high tone (´), low tone (`), rising tone (ˇ) and falling tone (^).

a Mid tone (sǐaŋ sǎaman): normal voice pitch:

    pay (ไป) to go   **maa** (มา) to come   **phɛɛŋ** (แพง) expensive

b High tone (sǐaŋ trii): higher than normal voice pitch:

    rót (รถ) car   **sɯ́ɯ** (ซื้อ) to buy   **lék** (เล็ก) small

c Low tone (sǐaŋ èek): lower than normal voice pitch:

    sìp (สิบ) ten   **càak** (จาก) from   **yày** (ใหญ่) big

d Rising tone (sǐaŋ càttawaa): starting from a lower than normal voice pitch with a distinctive rising contour:

    khɔ̌ɔŋ (ของ) of   **sǔay** (สวย) pretty   **phɔ̌ɔm** (ผอม) thin

e Falling tone (sǐaŋ thoo): starting from a higher than normal voice pitch with a distinctive falling contour:

    thîi (ที่) at   **chɔ̂ɔp** (ชอบ) to like   **phûut** (พูด) to speak

1.3.1   *Tone change*

There are a few common words which have a different tone in normal conversation to when pronounced slowly and deliberately in isolation. For example, **kháw** (เขา) 'he, she, they', **chán** (ฉัน) 'I' and **máy** (ไหม) (question particle) are all pronounced with a high tone in normal conversation but a rising tone when pronounced in isolation.

In one form of adjectival reduplication (see 6.4), the first element is pronounced with a high tone for the purpose of emphasis or intensification:

sǔay (สวย) beautiful

súay sǔay (สว๎ยสวย) so beautiful!

In certain situations tones may also change; the unstressed first syllable in a two-syllable word is usually pronounced with a mid tone (see 1.4), while when two syllables with rising tones follow one another, the first is often pronounced as a high tone:

náŋsɰ̌ɰ (หนังสือ) book

sɔ̌ɔŋ sǎam khon (สองสามคน) two or three people

1.4   Stress

In words of two syllables, unlike in English, it is the second syllable which is stressed. When the vowel in the first syllable is -a, it is normally reduced to -ə and in normal speech the tone is mid:

pratuu~prətuu (ประตู) door

sadùak~sədùak (สะดวก) convenient

When the vowel -aa occurs in both the first and second syllable, it is commonly shortened in the first syllable:

aahǎan~ahǎan (อาหาร) food

phaasǎa~phasǎa (ภาษา) language

Chapter 2

The writing system

Thai is written in a unique script. This has evolved from a script which originated in South India and was introduced into mainland South-East Asia during the fourth or fifth century AD. The neighbouring Lao and Cambodian scripts bear some close similarities to Thai. The first recorded example of Thai writing is widely believed to be a stone inscription found by the future King Mongkut (Rama IV, 1851–68) at Sukhothai in 1833, and dated 1283 AD. In this inscription, the author, King Ramkhamhaeng, records that he actually devised the script. In recent years there has been lively debate in academic circles about its authenticity; much of this can be found in Chamberlain (1991).

The Thai writing system is alphabetic. It is written across the page from left to right with no spaces between words; when spaces are used, they serve as punctuation markers, instead of commas or full stops. There is generally a close match between spelling and pronunciation. The following sections outline the key features of the Thai writing system:

2.1 Consonants

The Thai alphabet has forty-two consonants which are arranged according to the traditional Indian alphabetic order, beginning with velar stops, then palatals, dentals, bilabials and finally, sonorants.

All consonants are pronounced with an inherent -ɔɔ vowel sound. Each consonant has a name, rather like 'a-for-apple, b-for-bat', which children learn in school. For the foreign learner, knowing these names can be useful when asking how to spell a word, but is not necessary for learning to read.

Many consonant symbols change their pronunciation at the end of a word because of the very limited number of final consonant sounds that exist

11

in Thai (1.1.2); thus, the *letters* representing initial kh, c, ch, d, th, b, ph, s and f sounds are each channelled into one of just three possible *sounds* – k, p, t – when they occur at the end of a word. The following table lists the consonants in dictionary order with their names and pronunciations, both as initial and as final consonants:

Name		Initial	Final
ก	kɔɔ kày (chicken)	k	k
ข	khɔ̌ɔ khày (egg)	kh	k
ค	khɔɔ khwaay (buffalo)	kh	k
ฆ	khɔɔ rakhaŋ (bell)	kh	k
ง	ŋɔɔ ŋuu (snake)	ŋ	ŋ
จ	cɔɔ caan (plate)	c	t
ฉ	chɔ̌ɔ chìŋ (small cymbals)	ch	t
ช	chɔɔ cháaŋ (elephant)	ch	t
ซ	sɔɔ sôo (chain)	s	t
ฌ	chɔɔ (ka)chəə (tree)	ch	t
ญ	yɔɔ yǐŋ (girl)	y	n
ฎ	dɔɔ chádaa (theatrical crown)	d	t
ฏ	tɔɔ patàk (goad)	t	t
ฐ	thɔ̌ɔ thǎan (base)	th	t
ฑ	thɔɔ monthoo (Indra's Queen)	th	t
ฒ	thɔɔ thâw (old person)	th	t
ณ	nɔɔ neen (novice)	n	n
ด	dɔɔ dèk (child)	d	t
ต	tɔɔ tàw (turtle)	t	t
ถ	thɔ̌ɔ thǔŋ (bag)	th	t
ท	thɔɔ thahǎan (soldier)	th	t
ธ	thɔɔ thoŋ (flag)	th	t
น	nɔɔ nǔu (mouse)	n	n
บ	bɔɔ bay máay (leaf)	b	p
ป	pɔɔ plaa (fish)	p	p
ผ	phɔ̌ɔ phɨ̂ŋ (bee)	ph	p

ฝ	fɔ̌ɔ fǎa (lid)	**f**	**p**
พ	phɔɔ phaan (tray)	**ph**	**p**
ฟ	fɔɔ fan (tooth)	**f**	**p**
ภ	phɔɔ sǎmphaw (sailing ship)	**ph**	**p**
ม	mɔɔ máa (horse)	**m**	**m**
ย	yɔɔ yák (giant)	**y**	**y**
ร	rɔɔ rɨa (boat)	**r**	**n**
ล	lɔɔ liŋ (monkey)	**l**	**n**
ว	wɔɔ wɛ̌ɛn (ring)	**w**	**w**
ศ	sɔ̌ɔ sǎalaa (pavilion)	**s**	**t**
ษ	sɔ̌ɔ rɨsǐi (ascetic)	**s**	**t**
ส	sɔ̌ɔ sɨa (tiger)	**s**	**t**
ห	hɔ̌ɔ hìip (box)	**h**	**-**
ฬ	lɔɔ culaa (kite)	**l**	**n**
อ	ɔɔ àaŋ (bowl)	**'zero'***	**-**
ฮ	hɔɔ nók hûuk (owl)	**h**	**-**

*See 2.3.

The following table summarises the representation of final consonant
sounds; although there are theoretically fifteen ways of writing a final
-t sound, less than half of these are likely to be encountered in normal
usage.

Final consonant sound	Thai consonant symbol
-p	บ ป พ ภ ฟ
-t	ด ต ฎ ฏ จ ถ ฐ ท ธ ฑ ช ซ ศ ษ ส
-k	ก ข ค ฆ
-m	ม -ำ
-n	น ณ ญ ร ล ฬ
-ŋ	ง
-y	ย
-w	ว

2.2 Consonants by class

Thai consonants are divided into three classes: *high*, *mid* and *low*. The class of the initial consonant is one factor in determining the tone of a word or syllable. In order to be able to read, the learner has to memorise the class of each consonant; the easiest way to do this is to memorise the shorter lists of mid-class and high-class consonants so that everything not on those lists can be assumed to be low class.

Low class:	น	ม	ง	ร	ล	ย		ว		
	n	m	ŋ	r	l	y		w		
	ค	ช	ซ	ท	พ	ฟ				
	kh	ch	s	th	ph	f				
	ฆ	ฌ	ฑ	ญ	ณ					
	kh	th	ph	y	n					
	ฒ	ฬ	ฌ	ฬ	ฮ					
	ch	th	th	l	h					
Mid class:	ก	จ	ด	ต	บ	ป		อ	ฎ	ฏ
	k	c	d	t	b	p		zero d		t
High class:	ข	ฉ	ถ	ผ	ฝ	ศ ษ ส		ห	ฐ	
	kh	ch	th	ph	f	s		h	th	

2.3 Vowels

Vowel symbols can only be written in combination with a preceding consonant; they can appear after, before, above, or below a consonant, and even surrounding the consonant on three sides; in the following table, a dash is used to indicate the position of the consonant. When a word begins with a vowel sound, the 'zero' or 'glottal' consonant symbol is used. (Note that the Thai letter representing 'zero' consonant and the -ɔɔ vowel are identical.) Vowel length is important in Thai because it plays a part in determining the tone of a syllable; *short* vowels are indicated by a single letter in the transcription (e.g. -a, -i, -ɛ, -ə) and *long* vowels by two letters (e.g. -aa, -uu, -ɛɛ); the diphthongs -ua, -ia, -ɯa are regarded as long vowels. The following table lists the vowel symbols in alphabetical order:

-อ	**-ɔɔ**	เ-อะ	**-ə**
-ะ	**-a**	เ-ะ	**-e**
-ั-	**-a-**	เ-า	**-aw**
-ัว	**-ua**	เ-าะ	**-ɔ**
-า	**-aa**	เิ-	**-əə**
-ำ	**-am**	เี-ย	**-ia**
-ิ	**-i**	เี-ยะ	**-ia**
-ี	**-ii**	เี-อ	**-ɨa**
-ึ	**-ʉ**	แ--	**-ɛɛ**
-ื-	**-ʉʉ**	แี-	**-ɛ**
-ุ	**-u**	แ-ะ	**-ɛ**
-ู	**-uu**	โ-	**-oo**
เ-	**-ee**	โ-ะ	**-o**
เ็-	**-e**	ไ-	**-ay**
เ-ย	**-əəy**	ใ-	**-ay**
เ-อ	**-əə**		

2.4   Live syllables and dead syllables

Thai syllables are either *live* or *dead*. A live syllable (**kham pen**) ends with either a long vowel, or an **m, n, ŋ, w,** or **y** sound; a dead syllable (**kham taay**) ends with either a short vowel, or a **p, t,** or **k** sound:

Live syllables:	**maa**	**duu**	**wan**	**ram**	**kûŋ**	**aw**	**khǎay**
	มา	ดู	วัน	รำ	กุ้ง	เอา	ขาย

Dead syllables:	**tó**	**kà**	**dù**	**ráp**	**cùt**	**bɔ̀ɔk**
	โต๊ะ	กะ	ดุ	รับ	จุด	บอก

2.5 Tone rules

The tone of a syllable is determined by a combination of three different
factors: (i) the type of syllable (live or dead); (ii) the class of the initial
consonant (high, medium or low); and (iii) the length of the vowel (long
or short).

2.5.1 Dead syllables

The following table summarises tone rules for dead syllables with examples:

Initial consonant	Short vowel	Long vowel
Low class	HIGH TONE รัก **rák**	FALLING TONE มาก **mâak**
Mid class	LOW TONE ติด **tìt**	LOW TONE บาท **bàat**
High class	LOW TONE ขับ **khàp**	LOW TONE สอบ **sɔ̀ɔp**

2.5.2 Live syllables and tone marks

Live syllables with no tone mark are pronounced with a mid tone if the
initial consonant is either low class or mid class, but a rising tone if it
is a high-class consonant.

To represent live syllables with high, falling and low tones (such as the
words tɔ̂ŋ 'must' and mây 'not'), tone marks are used, which are written
above the initial consonant. The two most common tone marks are **máy
èek** (-) and **máy thoo** (̃). Unfortunately for the learner, because of a
radical change in the tone system that occurred centuries ago, these tone
marks do not indicate one specific tone each; again, it is the class of the
initial consonant which determines how the tone mark will be interpreted.

The following table summarises rules for live syllables with examples:

Initial consonant	(no tone mark)	**máy èek**	**máy thoo**
Low class	MID TONE มา maa	FALLING TONE ไม่ mây	HIGH TONE ม้า máa
Mid class	MID TONE ตาม taam	LOW TONE ต่อ tɔ̀ɔ	FALLING TONE ต้อง tɔ̂ŋ
High class	RISING TONE ขอ khɔ̌ɔ	LOW TONE ไข่ khày	FALLING TONE ข้าง khâaŋ

Two further tone marks, **máy trii** (-̋) and **máy càttawaa** (-̊) are also used, although they are much less common. The former always produces a high tone, the latter, always a rising tone.

โต๊ะ	เป๊ปซี่	เก๊
tó	**pépsîi**	**kée**
เดี๋ยว	จ๋า	ก๋วยเตี๋ยว
dǐaw	**cǎa**	**kǔay tǐaw**

2.5.3 Silent initial consonants: ห and อ

When the high-class consonant **ห** occurs before the low-class consonants, **ง, น, ม, ร, ย, ญ, ว, ล**, it is silent but has the effect of transforming the low-class consonants into high-class consonants; such words then follow the tone rules for words with initial high-class consonants (2.5.1, 2.5.2):

หยุด	หลอด	หนี	หญิง	หนึ่ง
yùt	**lɔ̀ɔt**	**nǐi**	**yǐŋ**	**nɯ̀ŋ**

The mid-class consonant **อ** occurs silently before the low-class consonant **ย** and has the effect of transforming the low-class consonant into a mid-class consonant. There are only four words in this category, all of which are pronounced with a low tone:

อยาก	อย่า	อย่าง	อยู่
yàak	**yàa**	**yàaŋ**	**yùu**

2.5.4 Consonant clusters

Consonant clusters occur only at the beginning of a syllable in Thai. In syllables beginning with a consonant cluster, the class of the first consonant in the cluster is used for determining the tone of the syllable. The following chart summarises possible consonant cluster sounds with examples:

kr- (กรอก **krɔ̀ɔk**)	kl- (ใกล้ **klây**)	kw- (กว้าง **kwâaŋ**)
khr- (ใคร **khray**)	khl- (คล้าย **khláay**)	khw- (ขวา **khwǎa**)
tr- (ตรวจ **trùat**)		
pr- (ปราบ **pràap**)	pl- (ปลุก **plùk**)	
phr- (พระ **phrá**)	phl- (พลาด **phlâat**)	

2.5.5 Unwritten vowels

2.5.5.1 Monosyllables

Syllables consisting of two consonants with no written vowel symbol are pronounced with an inherent o vowel sound:

คน	ยก	จบ	หก	หมด
khon	**yók**	**còp**	**hòk**	**mòt**

2.5.5.2 Two-syllable words

Many two-syllable words in Thai have an unwritten a vowel in the first syllable. The first syllable is unstressed and pronounced with a mid tone in normal speech; the tone of the second syllable is determined by the second consonant in the word (i.e. the initial consonant of the second syllable), unless that consonant is either ง, น, ม, ร, ย, ว, or ล, in which case the first consonant 'over-rules' it and determines the tone:

สบาย	สถาน	สภาพ	สนุก	ตลก
sabaay	**sathǎan**	**saphâap**	**sanùk**	**talòk**

There are a small number of words beginning with the letters บร-, in which the unwritten vowel sound is ɔ:

บริษัท	บริเวณ	บริการ	บริหาร	บริโภค
bɔrisàt	**bɔriween**	**bɔrikaan**	**bɔrihǎan**	**bɔriphôok**

2.6 Miscellaneous

2.6.1 Mismatch between spelling and pronunciation

Overall, the match between spelling and pronunciation in Thai is remarkably close; if you know the rules, you can almost guarantee that you will be able to read a word correctly. However, two common types of mismatch between spelling and normal pronunciation, are:

1 Tone suggested by the spelling is not reflected in pronunciation

Words written with rising tones but pronounced with high tones:

เขา (he, she, they) written **khǎw** but pronounced **kháw**

ฉัน (I) written **chǎn** but pronounced **chán**

ไหม (question particle) written **mǎy** but pronounced **máy**

Words written with falling tones but pronounced with low tones:

ประโยชน์ (advantage) written **prayôot** but pronounced **prayòot**

ประโยค (sentence) written **prayôok** but pronounced **prayòok**

ประวัติ (history) written **prawát** but pronounced **prawàt**

2 Vowel length in the written form is not reflected in pronunciation

Words written with long vowels but pronounced with short vowels:

ต้อง (must) written **tɔ̂ɔŋ** but pronounced **tɔ̂ŋ**

เงิน (money) written **ŋəən** but pronounced **ŋən**

ท่าน (you) written **thâan** but pronounced **thân**

Words written with short vowels but pronounced with long vowels:

ได้ (can, able to) written **dây** but pronounced **dâay**

เก้า (nine) written **kâw** but pronounced **kâaw**

ไม้ (wood) written **máy** but pronounced **máay**

2.6.2 Linker syllables and double-functioning consonants

A number of words that appear to consist of two syllables are joined by
a linker syllable consisting of the final consonant of the first syllable with
an unwritten **a** vowel between them:

สกปรก	คุณภาพ	ผลไม้	ราชการ
sòkkapròk	**khunnaphâap**	**phǒnlamáay**	**râatchakaan**

2.6.3 Silenced consonants

Thai words that have been borrowed from Sanskrit, Pali and English
usually try to retain as much of the original spelling as possible; as this
will often produce pronunciations that are impossible or misleading, a
'killer' symbol is placed above the redundant consonant to indicate that
it may be ignored:

เบียร์	เบอร์	จอห์น	เสาร์	อาทิตย์
bia	**bəə**	**cɔɔn**	**sǎw**	**aathít**

Sometimes the 'killer' sign, called **kaaran** in Thai, cancels out not only
the consonant above which it appears, but also the one immediately
preceding it:

จันทร์	ศาสตร์
can	**sàat**

Sometimes, even though there is no **kaaran** sign, the final consonant is
not pronounced:

บัตร	สมัคร
bàt	**samàk**

2.6.4 Silent final vowels

A number of words of Indic origin are spelt with a final short vowel
which is not pronounced:

ชาติ	ญาติ	เหตุ
châat	**yâat**	**hèet**

2.6.5	*Irregular ร*

The letter ร, normally pronounced as an inital **r** and final **n**, occurs in a
number of irregular combinations:

2.6.5.1	ทร-

These two letters together at the beginning of a word behave like low
class **s**:

ทราบ	ทราย	ทรง
sâap	**saay**	**soŋ**

2.6.5.2	สร-

The letter ร is not pronounced in words that begin with these two letters:

สร้าง	สรวง	สระ
sâaŋ	**sŭaŋ**	**sà**

2.6.5.3	Final ร

As a final consonant the letter ร is normally prounced **n**; in words where
there is no immediately preceding written vowel, it is pronounced **ɔɔn**:

พร	นคร	ละคร
phɔɔn	**nakhɔɔn**	**lakhɔɔn**

2.6.5.4	-รร

When the letters รร occur at the end of a syllable, they are pronounced
an; if they are followed by a final consonant they are pronounced **a**:

สรร	บรรทุก	กรรม	พรรค
săn	**banthúk**	**kam**	**phák**

2.6.5.5	จริง

The letter ร is ignored in the pronunciation of the word จริง (**ciŋ**).

The symbols ๆ and ฯ

The symbol ฯ indicates the abbreviation of a word and occurs most commonly in the word **kruŋthêep**, the Thai name for Bangkok. The symbol ๆ indicates the reduplication of the preceding word:

กรุงเทพฯ	เพื่อนๆ	เล็กๆ
kruŋthêep	**phûan phûan**	**lék lék**

Consonants . . . or what?

The four symbols below are listed in dictionaries as if they were consonants. Despite this, Thais tend to think of the Thai alphabet as having 44 consonants, including 2 obsolete consonants in addition to the 42 listed in 2.1, but excluding the symbols below.

ฤ	ฤๅ	ฦ	ฦๅ
rʉ	**rʉʉ**	**lʉ**	**lʉʉ**

The first symbol occurs in only a very small number of words (but including 'English' where it has the value **ri**), while the latter three are unlikely to be encountered.

อังกฤษ	**aŋkrìt**	English
ฤดู	**rʉduu**	season

Chapter 3

Nouns, classifiers and noun phrases

Nouns can be divided into two broad categories: proper nouns and common nouns.

3.1 Proper nouns

Proper nouns refer to unique things, such as personal names, place names and names of institutions.

3.1.1 Personal names

Names of individuals follow the same order as in English, with the personal name preceding the family name. People are addressed, referred to and known by their personal name rather than their family name; family names are used primarily for administrative purposes. Most Thais will also have a nickname, by which they will be known within the family and among friends.

The polite title **khun** is used before the personal name, and sometimes the nickname, to address both males and females of similar or higher status. Thus, Mr Suchart Boonsoong and Mrs Yupha Saibua will be known as **khun suchâat** and **khun yuphaa** respectively. Thais will often use **khun** followed by the surname when addressing Westerners in formal situations.

3.1.2 Place names

Individual place names, names of rivers, mountains and other geographical features, institutions, organisations, buildings, and so on, follow the noun identifying the type of place; an exception is Thailand's oldest university, Chulalongkorn University, which deliberately reverses the order:

caŋwàt nakhɔɔn phanom
จังหวัดนครพนม
Nakhorn Phanom Province

phâak iisǎan
ภาคอีสาน
North Eastern Region

mɛ̂ɛ náam câw phrayaa
แม่น้ำเจ้าพระยา
Chao Phraya River

mʉaŋ thay
เมืองไทย
Thailand

thanǒn sukhǔmwít
ถนนสุขุมวิท
Sukhumwit Road

sanǎam bin dɔɔn mʉaŋ
สนามบินดอนเมือง
Don Muang Airport

mahǎawítthayaalay thammasàat
มหาวิทยาลัยธรรมศาสตร์
Thammasat University

culaaloŋkɔɔn mahǎawítthayaalay
จุฬาลงกรณ์มหาวิทยาลัย
Chulalongkorn University

3.2 Common nouns

Common nouns are traditionally divided into concrete nouns, which are observable, such as 'house', and abstract nouns, which are not, such as 'love'.

Common nouns in Thai have a single fixed form. Unlike many European languages, no suffix is added to indicate plural or to show whether the noun is the grammatical subject or object in a sentence; nor are nouns classified by gender. The word **phûan** thus means either 'friend' or 'friends', depending on the context. Usually the context provides sufficient information for there to be no confusion. When it is necessary to be more specific, numbers or indefinite quantifier words, such as many, every, a few, can be used; a very small number of nouns may be reduplicated as a means of indicating plurality:

phǒm pay kàp phûan
ผมไปกับเพื่อน
I went with a friend/friends.

phǒm pay kàp phûan sɔ̌ɔŋ khon
ผมไปกับเพื่อนสองคน
I went with two friends.

phǒm pay kàp phûan lǎay khon
ผมไปกับเพื่อนหลายคน
I went with several friends.

phǒm pay kàp phûan phûan
ผมไปกับเพื่อนๆ
I went with friends.

3.3 Making new nouns

Common nouns make up the largest part of the language's vocabulary and are an ever-growing category. New nouns have, and continue to, come into the language through borrowing from other languages and from the Thai language's own means of generating new words, chiefly the process of compounding.

3.3.1 Borrowings

The Thai lexicon includes a considerable number of loan words, borrowed over the centuries from Khmer (Cambodian), the classical Indian languages, Sanskrit and Pali and, more recently, English. In some instances a word of Indic (Sanskrit or Pali) origin is used in preference to a 'pure' Thai word to convey a sense of politeness, refinement or formality:

Informal (Thai origin)		Formal (Indic origin)		
phŭa	ผัว	săamii	สามี	husband
mia	เมีย	phanrayaa	ภรรยา	wife
hŭa	หัว	sĭisà	ศีรษะ	head
mɯaŋ	เมือง	prathêet	ประเทศ	country
mǎa	หมา	sunák	สุนัข	dog

There has been a huge influx of English borrowings over the past fifty years, including scientific, technical and business terms and words associated with food, dress, arts, sports and other leisure activities. Thais' pronunciation of English loanwords will depend very much on their level of education and exposure to English; some English borrowings (e.g. páttìk, the 'uneducated' pronunciation of 'plastic', or bɔn, the abbreviated pronunciation of 'football') may be scarcely recognisable to an English native speaker when adapted to the Thai sound system and assigned tones. Here is just a tiny sample of English words in everyday use in Thai:

kɔ́p	กอล์ฟ	golf
phláastìk, páttìk	พลาสติก	plastic
fiim	ฟิล์ม	film
satɛ́m	แสตมป์	stamp
khɔmphiwtêə	คอมพิวเตอร์	computer
fútbɔn, bɔn	ฟุตบอล	football
ii-mee	อีเมล์	email
mɔɔtəəsay	มอเตอร์ไซค์	motorcycle

3.3.2 Compounds

Compounding involves joining two or more words together to make a new word. The first word or 'head noun' may be followed by either a 'noun attribute' or a 'verb attribute', which qualifies or restricts the meaning of the head noun; in some compounds, a verb attribute is followed by a grammatical object:

3.3.2.1	HEAD NOUN + NOUN ATTRIBUTE	

rót fay	รถไฟ	train (vehicle + fire)
ráan aahǎan	ร้านอาหาร	restaurant (shop + food)
ŋən dɯan	เงินเดือน	salary (money + month)
châŋ fay fáa	ช่างไฟฟ้า	electrician (mechanic + electricity)

3.3.2.2	HEAD NOUN + VERB (+ OBJECT) ATTRIBUTE	

nám khěŋ	น้ำแข็ง	ice (water + to be hard)
bòt rian	บทเรียน	lesson (text + to study)
kham nέnam	คำแนะนำ	introduction (word + introduce)
khon khàp rót	คนขับรถ	driver (person + to drive + car)
khrɯ̂aŋ sák phâa	เครื่องซักผ้า	washing machine (machine + to wash + clothes)

3.3.3 Some common head nouns

A number of head nouns occur either normally or exclusively in compounds; some common examples include the following:

3.3.3.1	**nák** ('one skilled in . . .') + VERB or NOUN	

nák sɯksǎa	นักศึกษา	student (**sɯksǎa** to study)
nák khǐan	นักเขียน	writer (**khǐan** to write)
nák kiilaa	นักกีฬา	sportsman, athlete (**kiilaa** sport)
nák thúrákìt	นักธุรกิจ	businessman (**thúrákìt** business)
nák náŋsɯ̌ɯphim	นักหนังสือพิมพ์	journalist (**náŋsɯ̌ɯphim** newspaper)

3.3.3.2	**phûu** ('one who . . .') + VERB (*but note last two examples with noun*)		

| **phûu yày** | ผู้ใหญ่ | adult | (**yày** to be big) |
| **phûu chîaw chaan** | ผู้เชี่ยวชาญ | expert | (**chîaw chaan** to be skilled) |

phûu ráay	ผู้ร้าย	criminal	(**ráay** to be bad)
phûu chaay	ผู้ชาย	man	(**chaay** male)
phûu yĭng	ผู้หญิง	woman	(**yĭng** female)

3.3.3.3 **bay** ('a sheet of paper') + VERB

bay ráp rɔɔŋ	ใบรับรอง	guarantee	(**ráp rɔɔŋ** to guarantee)
bay sănyaa	ใบสัญญา	contract	(**sănyaa** to promise)
bay anúyâat	ใบอนุญาต	permit	(**anúyâat** to permit)
bay khàp khìi	ใบขับขี่	driving licence	(**khàp khìi** to drive)
bay sèt ráp ŋən	ใบเสร็จรับเงิน	receipt	(**sèt ráp ŋən** finish – receive – money)

3.3.3.4 **rooŋ** ('a large building') + NOUN or VERB

rooŋ rót	โรงรถ	garage	(**rót** car)
rooŋ ŋaan	โรงงาน	factory	(**ŋaan** work)
rooŋ năŋ	โรงหนัง	cinema	(**năŋ** film, movie)
rooŋ rɛɛm	โรงแรม	hotel	(**rɛɛm** to stay overnight)
rooŋ rian	โรงเรียน	school	(**rian** to study)

3.3.3.5 **kaan** ('matters of . . .') + NOUN; **kaan** ('act of . . .') + VERB

kaan bâan	การบ้าน	homework	(**bâan** house, home)
kaan fay fáa	การไฟฟ้า	Electricity Authority	(**fay fáa** electricity)
kaan ŋən	การเงิน	finance	(**ŋən** money)
kaan mɯaŋ	การเมือง	politics	(**mɯaŋ** city, country)
kaan ráksăa	การรักษา	care, preservation	(**ráksăa** to care for)
kaan sɯksăa	การศึกษา	education	(**sɯksăa** to study)

kaan chûay lŭa	การช่วยเหลือ	assistance	(chûay lŭa to assist)
kaan dəən thaaŋ	การเดินทาง	travel	(dəən thaaŋ to travel)

The pattern **kaan** + VERB in many instances corresponds to the English gerund, or verbal noun, and it occurs commonly in written Thai:

kaan kin	การกิน	eating	(kin to eat)
kaan róp	การรบ	fighting	(róp to fight)
kaan rian	การเรียน	studying	(rian to study)
kaan phûut	การพูด	speaking	(phûut to speak)

In normal spoken Thai, however, the English gerund construction is more naturally conveyed simply by the verb without **kaan**:

kin taam ráan aahǎan phɛɛŋ
กินตามร้านอาหารแพง
Eating in restaurants is expensive.

rian náŋsɰ̌ɰ mây sanùk
เรียนหนังสือไม่สนุก
Studying is not fun.

phûut phaasǎa thay yâak
พูดภาษาไทยยาก
Speaking Thai is difficult.

3.3.3.6	**khwaam** (used to form abstract nouns) + VERB

khwaam rák	ความรัก	love	(rák to love)
khwaam rúu	ความรู้	knowledge	(rúu to know)
khwaam khít	ความคิด	idea	(khít to think)
khwaam sǎmrèt	ความสำเร็จ	success	(sǎmrèt to complete)
khwaam sùk	ความสุข	happiness	(sùk to be happy)

3.3.3.7 **thîi** ('person whom one . . ., place where . . .,
thing which . . .') + VERB

thîi prɯ̀ksǎa	ที่ปรึกษา	adviser	(**prɯ̀ksǎa** to consult)
thîi phɯ̂ŋ	ที่พึ่ง	benefactor	(**phɯ̂ŋ** to depend, rely on)
thîi rák	ที่รัก	darling	(**rák** to love)
thîi yùu	ที่อยู่	address	(**yùu** to live)
thîi tham ŋaan	ที่ทำงาน	place of work	(**tham ŋaan** to work)
thîi nâŋ	ที่นั่ง	seat	(**nâŋ** to sit)
thîi cɔ̀ɔt rót	ที่จอดรถ	car park	(**cɔ̀ɔt rót** to park – car)
thîi ralɯ́k	ที่ระลึก	souvenir	(**ralɯ́k** to think of)
thîi cɔ̀ kradàat	ที่เจาะกระดาษ	paper punch	(**cɔ̀ kradàat** to punch holes – paper)
thîi pə̀ət khùat	ที่เปิดขวด	bottle opener	(**pə̀ət khùat** to open – bottle)

3.3.4 *Co-ordinate compounds*

Two or more nouns can occur together to make a new noun in a 'co-ordinate compound' where the second noun does not modify the first:

phɔ̂ɔ mɛ̂ɛ	พ่อแม่	parents (father – mother)
phîi nɔ́ɔŋ	พี่น้อง	brothers and sisters (older sibling – younger sibling)
sɯ̂a phâa	เสื้อผ้า	clothes (upper garment – lower garment)

Often such compounds involve a four-syllable pattern, which may involve one or more of the following features: duplication of the first and third elements, internal rhyme, alliteration or the insertion of a meaningless syllable to preserve the rhythm.

pùu yâa taa yaay	ปู่ย่าตายาย	grandparents

(paternal grandfather – paternal grandmother – maternal grandfather – maternal grandmother)

chaaw rây chaaw naa   ชาวไร่ชาวนา   farmers
(people – dry rice field – people – wet rice field)

chaaw khǎw chaaw dɔɔy   ชาวเขาชาวดอย   mountain people
(people – hill – people – mountain)

nám phák nám rɛɛŋ   น้ำพักน้ำแรง   one's own effort/labour
(water – rest – water – energy)

khruu baa aacaan   ครูบาอาจารย์   teachers
(teacher – rhyming nonsense syllable – teacher)

wát waa aaraam   วัดวาอาราม   wats/temples
(temple – alliterative/rhyming nonsense syllable – temple buildings)

3.4   Noun phrases and classifiers

When a noun is accompanied by one or more modifying words, such as
'*three* cars', '*that* car' or '*the red* car', it is called a noun phrase. Noun
phrases in Thai frequently involve the use of a class of words called *classifiers*.

Classifiers are an obligatory component of noun phrases containing
numerals. In both English and Thai, uncountable nouns, such as rice,
beer and silk may be counted by the kilo, the bottle or the metre; in
Thai these measure words are regarded as classifiers. Thai differs from
English in that it uses classifiers for countable nouns such as 'friends',
'dogs' and 'books', where English simply places the number before the
noun. A rare exception in English is 'cattle' which are counted by the
'head'; 'head' functions like a Thai classifier. Every noun in Thai is counted
by a specific classifier; thus **khon** is used for counting people, **tua** for
animals and **lêm** for books:

phɤ̂an sɔ̌ɔŋ khon
เพื่อนสองคน
two friends (friends – two – classifier)

mǎa hâa tua
หมาห้าตัว
five dogs (dogs – five – classifier)

náŋsɯ̌ɯ sìp lêm
หนังสือสิบเล่ม
ten books (books – ten – classifier)

31

Some of the most common classifiers, and the nouns they are used with, are:

an	อัน	small objects
baan	บาน	doors, windows, mirrors
bay	ใบ	fruit, eggs, leaves, cups, bowls, slips of paper, documents
chabàp	ฉบับ	letters, newspapers, documents
chanít	ชนิด	types, kinds, sorts (of things)
chín	ชิ้น	pieces (of cake, meat, cloth, work)
chút	ชุด	sets of things
chûak	เชือก	elephants
dɔ̀ɔk	ดอก	flowers, keys
duaŋ	ดวง	stamps, stars, lamps, lights, hearts
fɔɔŋ	ฟอง	eggs
hèŋ	แห่ง	places
hɔ̀ɔ	ห่อ	packages, bundles
hɔ̂ŋ	ห้อง	rooms
khabuan	ขบวน	trains, processions
khan	คัน	vehicles, spoons, forks
khon	คน	people (except monks and royalty)
khɔ̂ɔ	ข้อ	items, clauses, points (e.g. in a contract or formal statement)
khûu	คู่	pairs (e.g. shoes, socks, married couples, but not trousers)
khrûaŋ	เครื่อง	telephones, TVs, radios, computers, etc.
lam	ลำ	boats, aeroplanes
lăŋ	หลัง	houses
lêm	เล่ม	books, knives
lɔ̀ɔt	หลอด	light bulbs, tubes (e.g. toothpaste)
lûuk	ลูก	fruit, balls
mét	เม็ด	seeds, pills, buttons

muan	มวน	cigarettes, cigars
múan	ม้วน	cassettes, videos, reels of film, rolls of paper
oŋ	องค์	members of royalty, Buddha images
phɛ̀n	แผ่น	flat objects, sheets of paper, records
rûup	รูป	pictures, monks
rɯan	เรือน	clocks, watches
rɯ̂aŋ	เรื่อง	stories
sǎay	สาย	bus routes, railway lines, roads
sên	เส้น	long, thin items; strands of hair, necklaces, noodles
sîi	ซี่	teeth
tôn	ต้น	trees, plants
tua	ตัว	animals, chairs, tables, items of clothing, including trousers
yàaŋ	อย่าง	types, kinds, sorts (of things)

In addition, measure words such as kilo, inch and month, and containers such as bottle, bowl and bag also function as classifiers.

Classifiers occur not only with cardinal numbers, but also with other quantifiers (ordinal numbers, indefinite quantifiers and 'how many?'), demonstratives ('this', 'that', 'these', 'those' and 'which?') and adjectives.

3.5 Word order in noun phrases

The following list is not exhaustive but covers the most common patterns of noun phrase:

3.5.1 NOUN + CARDINAL NUMBER + CLASSIFIER

For cardinal numbers, see 13.1.

lûuk sǎam khon
ลูกสามคน
three children

bâan sìi lăŋ
บ้านสี่หลัง
four houses

náŋsɰ̌ɰ hòk lêm
หนังสือหกเล่ม
six books

The word **nɯ̀ŋ** (one) can occur either before the classifier or after it; when it occurs before the classifier it functions as the numeral 'one', and when it occurs after the classifier it can be treated as the indefinite article 'a', describing the noun:

lûuk nɯ̀ŋ khon
ลูกหนึ่งคน
one child

lûuk khon nɯ̀ŋ
ลูกคนหนึ่ง
a child

3.5.2 NOUN + QUANTIFIER + CLASSIFIER

For quantifiers, see 13.12; note that some quantifiers do not occur with classifiers.

faràŋ baaŋ khon
ฝรั่งบางคน
some 'farangs' (Westerners)

plaa thúk chanít
ปลาทุกชนิด
every kind of fish

còtmăay mây kìi chabàp
จดหมายไม่กี่ฉบับ
not many letters

3.5.3 NOUN + CLASSIFIER + ORDINAL NUMBER

For ordinal numbers, see 13.3.

lûuk khon thîi săam
ลูกคนที่สาม
the third child

bâan lăŋ thîi sɔ̆ɔŋ
บ้านหลังที่สอง
the second house

náŋsɯ̆ɯ lêm rɛ̂ɛk
หนังสือเล่มแรก
the first book

NOUN + CLASSIFIER + DEMONSTRATIVE

Demonstratives are words like **níi** ('this/these'), **nán** ('that/those'), **nóon** ('that/those over there') and the question word **năy?** ('which?'):

lûuk khon níi
ลูกคนนี้
this child

sɯ̂a tua nán
เสื้อตัวนั้น
that blouse

bâan lăŋ nóon
บ้านหลังโน้น
that house over there

náŋsɯ̆ɯ lêm năy?
หนังสือเล่มไหน
which book?

The noun is often dropped in spoken Thai when the context is unambiguous, as in the response below:

aw sɯ̂a tua năy?
เอาเสื้อตัวไหน
Which blouse do you want?

– tua nán
– ตัวนั้น
– That one.

The classifier is also often dropped in spoken Thai:

sɯ̂a nán mây sŭay
เสื้อนั้นไม่สวย
That blouse isn't pretty.

3.5.5 NOUN + CARDINAL NUMBER + CLASSIFIER + DEMONSTRATIVE

lûuk sǎam khon níi
ลูกสามคนนี้
these three children

sɨ̂a sɔ̌ɔŋ tua nán
เสื้อสองตัวนั้น
those two blouses

3.5.6 NOUN + ADJECTIVE

aahǎan phèt
อาหารเผ็ด
spicy food

náŋsɨ̌ɨ kàw
หนังสือเก่า
an old book

bâan yày
บ้านใหญ่
a big house

3.5.7 NOUN + ADJECTIVE + CLASSIFIER + DEMONSTRATIVE

náŋsɨ̌ɨ kàw lêm nán
หนังสือเก่าเล่มนั้น
that old book

bâan yày lǎŋ nán
บ้านใหญ่หลังนั้น
that big house

3.5.8 NOUN + ADJECTIVE + CARDINAL NUMBER + CLASSIFIER (+ DEMONSTRATIVE)

náŋsɨ̌ɨ kàw sɔ̌ɔŋ lêm (níi)
หนังสือเก่าสองเล่ม(นี้)
(these) two old books

bâan yày hâa lăŋ (nán)
บ้านใหญ่ห้าหลัง(นั้น)
(those) five big houses

3.5.9 NOUN + ADJECTIVE + CLASSIFIER + ORDINAL NUMBER

náŋsɯ̆ɯ kàw lêm thîi sɔ̆ɔŋ
หนังสือเก่าเล่มที่สอง
the second old book

bâan yày lăŋ thîi sǎam
บ้านใหญ่หลังที่สาม
the third big house

3.5.10 NOUN + CLASSIFIER + ADJECTIVE

This pattern is used to distinguish the noun referred to from other members of the same class:

sɯ̂a tua mày
เสื้อตัวใหม่
the new shirt

náŋsɯ̆ɯ lêm kàw
หนังสือเล่มเก่า
the old book

3.5.11 NOUN + NOUN

Some nouns can be used adjectivally to modify the preceding noun:

tamrùat phûu sɔ̀ɔp sǔan
ตำรวจผู้สอบสวน
the investigating police officer
(policeman – one who – investigate)

khâarâatchakaan chán phûu yày
ข้าราชการชั้นผู้ใหญ่
a high-ranking civil servant
(civil servant – rank – senior person)

3.5.12 NOUN + (khɔ̌ɔŋ) + POSSESSOR

In possessive phrases, **khɔ̌ɔŋ** ('of') is optional and is very frequently omitted:

bâan (khɔ̌ɔŋ) chán
บ้าน(ของ)ฉัน
my house

lûuk (khɔ̌ɔŋ) kháw
ลูก(ของ)เขา
his child

Chapter 4

Pronouns

4.1 Personal pronouns: basics

Thai has many more personal pronouns than English; age, social status, gender, the relationship between the speakers, the formality of the situation and individual personality all play a part in helping a Thai to decide the most appropriate way to refer to him/herself and address and refer to others in any situation.

Kin terms (aunt, older brother), status/occupation terms (teacher, doctor) and personal names or nicknames are also commonly used as personal pronouns.

As a starting point for learners, the personal pronoun system can be simplified to the following:

phǒm	ผม	I/me (male)
chán	ฉัน	I/me (female; informal)
dichán	ดิฉัน	I/me (female; formal)
raw	เรา	we/us
khun	คุณ	you (sing. and plur.)
thân	ท่าน	you (sing. and plur.); he/him, she/her, they/them. To address or refer to people of significantly higher social status
kháw	เขา	he/him; she/her; they/them
man	มัน	it

Note that male and female speakers use a different word for 'I/me', while a single third person pronoun in Thai covers 'he/him', 'she/her', 'they/them'. Usage of these and other pronouns is discussed in more detail in the next section.

Pronouns have a single form for subject and object:

phǒm chɔ̂ɔp kháw
ผมชอบเขา
I like him/her/them.

kháw chɔ̂ɔp phǒm
เขาชอบผม
He/she/they like(s) me.

The plural reference of a pronoun can be clarified or made explicit by (a) a number or other quantifier expression or (b) the pluralizer word phûak ('group'):

raw sǎam khon
เราสามคน
the three of us

khun tháŋ sɔ̌ɔŋ (khon)
คุณทั้งสอง(คน)
the two/both of you

kháw tháŋ lǎay
เขาทั้งหลาย
all of them

phûak raw
พวกเรา
we, us, 'us lot'

Pronouns are frequently omitted when it is clear from the context who is speaking, being addressed or being referred to:

pay phrûŋ níi
ไปพรุ่งนี้
I'm/we're/he's/she's/they're going tomorrow. (lit. go tomorrow)

chɔ̂ɔp máy?
ชอบไหม
Do you/do they/does he/she like it? (lit. like + question particle)

In these and many of the other examples in this book, an arbitrary choice of pronoun is supplied in the English translation. Since pronouns reflect relative status and intimacy, a speaker can, by omission, avoid the possibility of using an inappropriate pronoun. But the omission of pronouns is not simply a strategy for the cautious to avoid linguistic *faux pas*; it is also a means of denying or avoiding the behavioural or attitudinal expectations of intimacy or deference implicit in the use of any pronoun.

4.1.1 | *More personal pronouns*

Thais will use a much wider range of pronouns than those given in the previous section. Some of these are given below with an indication of whether they are specifically male (M) or female (F) pronouns and the context in which they are used; certain first person pronouns are normally 'paired' with a specific second person pronoun. Note that some pronouns (e.g. **thân** and **thəə**) function as both second and third person pronouns:

phǒm	ผม	M	1st person; general pronoun that can be used in most situations, ranging from polite to intimate; not used with young children.
kraphǒm	กระผม	M	1st person; highly deferential.
dichán	ดิฉัน	F	1st person; very formal, often avoided because it creates distance between speaker and addressee.
chán	ฉัน	M/F	1st person; commonly used by female speakers as a less formal, more friendly variant of **dichán**; also used by males as an expression of intimacy, when it is paired with **thəə**, and when speaking to children.
khâaphacâw	ข้าพเจ้า	M/F	1st person pronoun used formally in public statements and official documents.
raw	เรา	M /F	1st person plural; also used as 1st person singular pronoun in informal speech by both males and females.

nŭu	หนู	M/F	1st/2nd person pronoun used by children talking to adults; literally means 'rat'; used by girls and young women to superiors, for example, female students to teachers, secretaries to bosses, etc.
kuu	กู	M/F	1st person pronoun used mainly by males as a male-bonding pronoun in informal situations, such as drinking and brothel visits; also used to show anger; paired with **mʉŋ** (มึง).
úa	อั๊ว	M	1st person pronoun, from Teochiu dialect of Chinese; used mainly by males with close friends as an informal pronoun; paired with **lʉ́ʉ** (ลื้อ).
khâa	ข้า	M	1st person pronoun; used mainly by males with close friends as an informal pronoun; paired with **eŋ** (เอ็ง).
ay	ไอ	M/F	1st person pronoun; from English 'I'; infomal, paired with **yuu** (ยู).
kan	กัน	M	1st person pronoun; used among close male friends; paired with **kɛɛ** (แก).
khun	คุณ	M/F	2nd person, sing. and plur.; polite, formal use among equals; also used as a polite title before names, kin terms and certain occupations.
thân	ท่าน	M/F	2nd/3rd person, sing. and plur.; to address or refer to people of significantly higher social status; also used as a deferential title with certain high status positions.
thəə	เธอ	M/F	2nd/3rd person, sing. and plur.; as a 2nd person pronoun it is paired with **chán** and signals a relationship of closeness; as a 3rd person pronoun it usually refers to a female.

kháw	เขา	M/F	3rd person, sing. and plur.; also a 1st person pronoun, used among girls and between husband and wife, when it is paired with **tua** (ตัว).
kɛɛ	แก	M/F	3rd person, sing. and plur.; also as a 2nd person intimate pronoun among members of the same sex, when it is paired with **chán** (F) or **kan** (M).
man	มัน	–	'it'; regarded as unrefined and often avoided in polite, formal speech and writing; used widely in informal situations – including to refer to people, either derogatively or familiarly.

4.1.2 Kin terms as personal pronouns

Kin terms are commonly used as pronouns. A father, for example, will refer to himself as **phɔ̂ɔ** ('father') rather than **phǒm** ('I') when talking to his son and address his son as **lûuk** ('child') rather than **khun** ('you'):

phɔ̂ɔ mây chɔ̂ɔp
พ่อไม่ชอบ
I (father speaking) don't like it.

lûuk pay nǎy?
ลูกไปไหน
Where are you (parent addressing child) going?

Kin terms can be used as first, second or third person pronouns; thus, depending on the context, the sentence **phɔ̂ɔ maw lɛ́ɛw** can mean (a) I (father speaking) am drunk; (b) You (addressing father) are drunk; or (c) He (referring to father) is drunk.

The use of kin terms extends to include those who are not blood relations; by addressing an elderly man as **luŋ** ('uncle') or a friend or colleague as **phîi** ('older brother/sister') the speaker immediately creates an atmosphere of congeniality. Thus **phîi** has a particularly wide range of use, which includes wives addressing their husbands, service-industry workers addressing customers and complete strangers striking up a conversation with someone older.

Kin terms are often followed by personal names or nicknames (see 4.1.3). They can also be preceded by the polite title **khun** as a sign of further respect; thus children may address and refer to their parents as **khun phɔ̂ɔ** and **khun mɛ̂ɛ** (or collectively, as **khun phɔ̂ɔ khun mɛ̂ɛ**) and address a younger friend of their father as **khun aa** ('uncle/aunt').

The kin terms most commonly used as personal pronouns are:

phɔ̂ɔ	พ่อ	father
mɛ̂ɛ	แม่	mother
phîi	พี่	older brother/sister
nɔ́ɔŋ	น้อง	younger brother/sister
lûuk	ลูก	child
lǎan	หลาน	grandchild; niece/nephew
pâa	ป้า	aunt (older sister of parents)
luŋ	ลุง	uncle (older brother of parents)
náa	น้า	aunt/uncle (younger brother/sister of mother)
aa	อา	aunt/uncle (younger brother/sister of father)
pùu	ปู่	grandfather (father's father)
yâa	ย่า	grandmother (father's mother)
taa	ตา	grandfather (mother's father)
yaay	ยาย	grandmother (mother's mother)

4.1.3 | Personal names as personal pronouns

Personal names or nicknames are also commonly used as personal pronouns. Using one's name or more commonly, nickname instead of an 'I' word is characteristic of female speech but much less common among men. When used as second or third person pronouns, names and nick-names can be preceded by **khun** or a kin term, such as **phîi**, as a sign of deference:

tɔ̂y mây sâap khâ
ต้อยไม่ทราบค่ะ
I (Toi speaking) don't know.

khun suwannii wâaŋ máy?

คุณสุวรรณีว่างไหม

Are you (addressing Suwannee) free?

khun ûan klàp bâan lɛ́ɛw

คุณอ้วนกลับบ้านแล้ว

(Khun) Uan has gone home.

phîi sù ca pay dûay máy?

พี่สุจะไปด้วยไหม

Is (older sister) Su going too?

4.1.4 Occupation and status terms as personal pronouns

A number of occupation terms are commonly used instead of pronouns. In the medical and education worlds the following occupation terms are used not only as second or third person pronouns, when addressing or referring to individuals, but also as first person pronouns to mean 'I':

aacaan	อาจารย์	teacher, university lecturer
khruu	ครู	teacher
mɔ̌ɔ	หมอ	doctor
phayabaan	พยาบาล	nurse

Note that when addressing teachers or doctors, the polite title **khun** commonly precedes **khruu** and **mɔ̌ɔ**.

Taxi drivers, however, do not refer to themselves as **théksîi**; the following occupation terms are used only as second and third person pronouns:

krapǎw	กระเป๋า	bus conductor
sǎamlɔ́ɔ	สามล้อ	pedicab driver
théksîi	แท็กซี่	taxi driver
túk túk	ตุ๊กตุ๊ก	motorized pedicab driver

The occupants of certain high-ranking positions, such as ambassadors, director generals, rectors, ministers and prime ministers are often addressed and referred to using the deferential title **thân** before their position, or an abbreviated form of it:

| thân thûut | ท่านทูต | Ambassador |
| thân àthíbɔdii | ท่านอธิบดี | Director General |

thân àthíkaan	ท่านอธิการฯ	(University) Rector
thân rátthamontrii	ท่านรัฐมนตรี	Minister
thân naayók	ท่านนายกฯ	Prime Minister

When speaking to monks or royalty, further complicated sets of pronouns are used, which vary according the ecclesiastical or royal rank of the individual. The learner needs to be aware that an ordinary monk will address a non-monk as **yoom** and will refer to himself as **àattamaa**. The non-monk should use the polite formal first person pronouns **phǒm**, (males) or **dichán** (females) and address or refer to the monk as **lǔaŋ phɔ̌ɔ** or **lǔaŋ taa** (for older monks), **lǔaŋ phîi** or **lǔaŋ náa** (for younger monks), or simply by the deferential second person pronoun, **thân**:

àattamaa	อาตมา	I (monk speaking)
yoom	โยม	you (monk speaking)
lǔaŋ phɔ̌ɔ	หลวงพ่อ	you/he (layman addressing/referring to a monk)
lǔaŋ phîi	หลวงพี่	you/he (layman addressing/referring to a monk)

Using the complex system of royal pronouns correctly is a daunting prospect even for the vast majority of educated Thais. At the simplest level, one should refer to oneself as **khâaphraphútthacâw** ('Your Majesty's servant') when addressing the King or other high-ranking members of royalty, and use **tâayfàalaɔɔŋthúliiphrabàat** as a second person pronoun to the King and **tâayfàalaɔɔŋphrabàat** to other high-ranking members of royalty; both terms can be translated as 'dust under sole of royal foot'. Members of royalty, unlike monks, do not use special pronouns when talking to ordinary people.

khâaphraphútthacâw
ข้าพระพุทธเจ้า
I (to King)

tâayfàalaɔɔŋthúliiphrabàat
ใต้ฝ่าละอองธุลีพระบาท
you (to King)

tâayfàalaɔɔŋphrabàat
ใต้ฝ่าละอองพระบาท
you (to high-ranking royalty)

4.2 Reflexive pronouns

The reflexive pronoun, **tua** ('body') is used with first, second and third persons. It occurs in such verbs as:

ciam tua	เจียมตัว	to be self-effacing
khǎay tua	ขายตัว	to sell oneself
khayǎay tua	ขยายตัว	to expand
khɔ̌ɔ tua	ขอตัว	to excuse oneself
lên tua	เล่นตัว	to play hard to get
lʉʉm tua	ลืมตัว	to forget oneself
pràp tua	ปรับตัว	to adapt oneself
rúu tua	รู้ตัว	to be aware
sanǒǝ tua	เสนอตัว	to put oneself forward
sǐa tua	เสียตัว	to lose one's virginity
sǐa salà tua	เสียสละตัว	to sacrifice oneself
sɔ̂ɔn tua	ซ่อนตัว	to hide oneself
tèŋ tua	แต่งตัว	to get dressed
triam tua	เตรียมตัว	to prepare oneself
thɔ̀ɔm tua	ถ่อมตัว	to be self-effacing
thʉ̌ʉ tua	ถือตัว	to be aloof

The verb 'to kill oneself/commit suicide' is irregular, translating literally as 'kill – body/self – dead':

khâa tua taay ฆ่าตัวตาย to commit suicide

For a smaller category of verbs, the reflexive pronoun must be followed by the emphatic pronoun **eeŋ** ('self'):

chûay tua eeŋ	ช่วยตัวเอง	to help oneself
duu lɛɛ tua eeŋ	ดูแลตัวเอง	to look after oneself
mân cay tua eeŋ	มั่นใจตัวเอง	to be self-confident
mɔɔŋ tua eeŋ	มองตัวเอง	to look at oneself

phuum cay tua eeŋ	ภูมิใจตัวเอง	to be proud of oneself
phûŋ tua eeŋ	พึ่งตัวเอง	to rely on oneself
thǎam tua eeŋ	ถามตัวเอง	to ask oneself
wâat rûup tua eeŋ	วาดรูปตัวเอง	to draw a picture of oneself

The idea of doing something 'by oneself' uses either **dûay** ('by') **tua eeŋ** or **dûay ton eeŋ**; the latter is less common in speech and carries a slightly formal or literary flavour:

phǒm sɔ̂ɔm rót dûay tua eeŋ
ผมซ่อมรถด้วยตัวเอง
I mended the car by myself.

raw tham dûay tua eeŋ
เราทำด้วยตัวเอง
We did it by ourselves.

kháw rian dûay ton eeŋ
เขาเรียนด้วยตนเอง
He studied by himself.

4.3 Emphatic pronoun

The emphatic pronoun **eeŋ** ('self') is used with first, second and third persons; it occurs in the following patterns, each conveying a slightly different shade of emphasis:

4.3.1 PERSONAL PRONOUN + eeŋ + VERB

phǒm eeŋ tham
ผมเองทำ
I myself did it.

4.3.2 PERSONAL PRONOUN + VERB + eeŋ

phǒm tham eeŋ
ผมทำเอง
I did it myself.

4.3.3   PERSONAL PRONOUN + eeŋ + pen khon + VERB

phǒm eeŋ pen khon tham
ผมเองเป็นคนทำ
I myself was the one who did it.

4.3.4   tua + PERSONAL PRONOUN + eeŋ + VERB

tua phǒm eeŋ tham
ตัวผมเองทำ
I myself did it.

eeŋ also occurs after demonstratives to convey the sense of 'the very same (one)', 'precisely':

phɯ̂an khon níi eeŋ
เพื่อนคนนี้เอง
this very friend

wan nán eeŋ
วันนั้นเอง
that very day

dǐaw níi eeŋ
เดี๋ยวนี้เอง
right now

sǎam rɔ́ɔy bàat thâwnán eeŋ
สามร้อยบาทเท่านั้นเอง
just three hundred baht

4.4   Reciprocal: 'each other'

The reciprocal pronoun 'each other/one another' is expressed by the pattern SUBJECT + VERB (PHRASE) + kan ('together'):

kháw rák kan
เขารักกัน
They love each other.

raw tɔ̂ŋ chûay kan
เราต้องช่วยกัน
We must help one another.

4.5 Possessive pronouns

The possessive pronouns 'mine', 'yours', 'his', etc. are formed using khɔ̌ɔŋ ('of') + PERSONAL PRONOUN:

khɔ̌ɔŋ chán
ของฉัน
Mine.

khɔ̌ɔŋ khun sǔay
ของคุณสวย
Yours is pretty.

rót nán khɔ̌ɔŋ kháw
รถนั้นของเขา
That car is his.

4.6 Demonstrative pronouns

There are three demonstrative pronouns, nîi ('this one'), nân ('that one') and nôon – sometimes pronounced nûun – ('that one over there'):

nîi mây sǔay
นี่ไม่สวย
This one isn't pretty.

nôon khɔ̌ɔŋ khray?
โน่นของใคร
Whose is that one over there?

Demonstrative pronouns also occur in these common idiomatic expressions:

nîi yaŋŋay
นี่ยังไง
Here you are (when giving someone something).

nân ná sì
นั่นนะสิ
Exactly! That's right!

tɛ̀ɛ nân lɛ̀
แต่นั่นแหละ
even so; nevertheless

4.7 Interrogative pronouns

For the use of interrogative pronouns (listed below) in questions, see 12.2:

khray?	ใคร	who?
aray?	อะไร	what?
mûaràay?	เมื่อไร	when?
thîi năy?	ที่ไหน	where?
năy?	ไหน	which?
yaŋŋay?	อย่างไร	how?
thâwràay?	เท่าไร	how much?

4.8 Indefinite pronouns

Interrogative pronouns also act as the indefinite pronouns, 'somebody', 'something', 'somewhere', etc.

4.8.1 'Somebody', 'anybody', 'nobody'

khray as an indefinite pronoun means 'somebody', 'anybody', 'whoever'; **mây mii khray** ('there is not anyone') means 'nobody':

phŏm khuy kàp khray khon nèŋ
ผมคุยกับใครคนหนึ่ง
I chatted to somebody.

chán mây dây phop khray
ฉันไม่ได้พบใคร
I didn't meet anybody.

mii khray ca kin máy?
มีใครจะกินไหม
Is anybody going to eat?

khray sèt pay dâay
ใครเสร็จไปได้
Whoever is finished can go.

mây mii khray rúu
ไม่มีใครรู้
Nobody knows.

'Something', 'anything', 'nothing'

aray as an indefinite pronoun means 'something', 'anything', 'whatever', **mây mii aray** ('there is not anything') means 'nothing':

kháw yàak séé aray baaŋ yàaŋ
เขาอยากซื้ออะไรบางอยาง
She wants to buy something.

khun yàak kin aray máy?
คุณอยากกินอะไรไหม
Do you want to eat anything?

phǒm mây dây phûut aray
ผมไม่ได้พูดอะไร
I didn't say anything.

mây mii aray nâa sǒn cay
ไม่มีอะไรน่าสนใจ
There is nothing interesting.

'Whenever'

mêarày as an indefinite pronoun means 'whenever'; it can occur either before or after the verb in the first clause:

kin mêarày kô thóoŋ sǐa
กินเมื่อไรก็ท้องเสีย
Whenever I eat it, I get diarrhoea.

mêarày wâaŋ thoo maa hǎa
เมื่อไรว่างโทรมาหา
Whenever you are free, phone me.

'Somewhere', 'anywhere', 'nowhere'

thîi nǎy as an indefinite pronoun means 'somewhere', 'anywhere', 'wherever'; note that when it immediately follows the verb **pay** ('to go') the word **thîi** is frequently dropped:

chán yàak pay yùu thîi nǎy thîi ŋîap ŋîap

ฉันอยากไปอยู่ที่ไหนที่เงียบ ๆ

I want to go and live somewhere quietish.

yàak pay nǎy máy?

อยากไปไหนไหม

Do you want to go anywhere?

mây yàak pay nǎy

ไม่อยากไปไหน

I don't want to go anywhere.

'Whichever'

nǎy as an indefinite pronoun means 'whichever one'; it always follows a classifier and normally occurs with **kɔ̂ dâay** (4.8.7):

phǒm ca sɯ́ɯ an nǎy kɔ̂ dâay thîi mây phɛɛŋ

ผมจะซื้ออันไหนก็ได้ที่ไม่แพง

I'll buy whichever one is not expensive.

'However'

yaŋŋay as an indefinite pronoun means 'however', 'whatever way'; it always follows a verb:

tham yaŋŋay kɔ̂ phlâat thúk thii

ทำอย่างไรก็พลาดทุกที

However I do it, I always make a mistake.

Indefinite pronouns with **kɔ̂ dâay**

Indefinite pronouns occur before **kɔ̂ dâay** to show amenability or indifference, as in expressions such as 'whoever/whenever/whatever you like'. Note that the vowel in **dâay** is long although it is written in Thai script as a short vowel:

sàŋ aray kɔ̂ dâay

สั่งอะไรก็ได้

Order whatever you like.

bɔ̀ɔk khray kɔ̂ dâay
บอกใครก็ได้
Tell whoever you like.

raw phóp kan mʉ̂aràay kɔ̂ dâay
เราพบกันเมื่อไรก็ได้
We'll meet whenever you like.

raw pay nǎy kɔ̂ dâay
เราไปไหนก็ได้
We can go anywhere you like.

sʉ́ʉ an nǎy kɔ̂ dâay
ซื้ออันไหนก็ได้
Buy whichever one you like.

kin yaŋŋay kɔ̂ dâay
กินอย่างไรก็ได้
You can eat it however you like.

hây thâwràay kɔ̂ dâay
ให้เท่าไรก็ได้
You can give however much you like.

4.9 Relative pronouns

A single relative pronoun **thîi** is used to refer to people, places and things:

kháw pen ̥khon thîi càay
เขาเป็นคนที่จ่าย
He is the one who paid.

b̥âan thîi ̥kháw yùu lék
บ้านที่เขาอยู่เล็ก
The house where they live is small.

klûay thîi ̥kháw sʉ́ʉ phɛɛŋ
กล้วยที่เขาซื้อแพง
The bananas which she bought are expensive.

sʉ̂ŋ can be used interchangeably with **thîi** but it is a rather formal-sounding word and much less common in spoken Thai:

cháaŋ sʉ̂ŋ mii sɔ̌ɔŋ praphêet . . .
ช้างซึ่งมีสองประเภท . . .
Elephants, of which there are two kinds, . . .

an also functions rather like a relative pronoun, in a formal, stylised linking of noun and adjective (or stative verb); it cannot link a noun and an action verb:

rót an sǔay ŋaam
รถอันสวยงาม
a beautiful car

lôok an kwâaŋ yày
โลกอันกว้างใหญ่
the wide world

ŋaan an nàk nǎa
งานอันหนักหนา
a heavy task

Chapter 5

Verbs

Thai is a verb-oriented language, often using verbs where English uses nouns (3.3.3.5) or prepositions. Verbs have a single form: they are not inflected for number or tense. Thus **pay** can mean 'go', 'went', 'will go', etc.; ambiguity can be avoided by the addition of time expressions, such as 'yesterday' or 'next week' or auxiliary verbs and particles (5.3), but often the context alone is sufficient to clarify the situation. A common feature of Thai is verb serialization (5.13).

5.1 The verb 'to be'

Thai uses several different verbs to translate English 'is/are', 'was/were', etc; the most important are **pen, khɯɯ, mii** and **yùu**.

5.1.1 pen

When **pen** means 'to be' it is always followed by a noun or noun phrase; it cannot be followed by an adjective (see 5.2):

kháw pen phɯ̂an
เขาเป็นเพื่อน
He is a friend.

mɛ̂ɛ pen khon thay
แม่เป็นคนไทย
My mother is Thai.

phîi sǎaw pen khruu
พี่สาวเป็นครู
Her sister is a teacher.

When **pen** means 'to be', unlike other verbs, it cannot be negated by placing the negative word **mây** immediately before it. Instead, the negative form 'is not' is either **mây châay** or **mây dâay pen**; of these, the former is neutral in tone, while the latter conveys the sense of contradicting a spoken or unspoken assumption:

kháw mây châay khon ameerikan
เขาไม่ใช่คนอเมริกัน
He isn't American.

mây châay phǒm
ไม่ใช่ผม
It wasn't me.

kháw mây dâay pen phûan
เขาไม่ได้เป็นเพื่อน
He's not a friend.

For a summary of different usages of **pen**, see Appendix 2.

5.1.2 **khɯɯ**

khɯɯ means 'is equal to' or 'namely' and it is used when giving explanations, clarifications and definitions; it is also used as a hesitation device. **khɯɯ** does not occur in the negative:

sǎam bùak kàp sìi khɯɯ cèt
สามบวกกับสี่คือเจ็ด
Three plus four is seven.

mii panhǎa sǎam yàaŋ khɯɯ . . .
มีปัญหาสามอย่างคือ . . .
There are three problems, namely . . .

kham mɯaŋ khɯɯ phaasǎa thîi khon chiaŋmày phûut
คำเมืองคือภาษาที่คนเชียงใหม่พูด
'Kham Muang' is the language people in Chiangmai speak.

khɯɯ yàaŋ níi ná . . .
คืออย่างนี้นะ
It's like this, right?

In some instances, such as introductions and identifying people in photographs, **pen** and **khʉʉ** are interchangeable:

nîi khʉʉ/pen săamii chán
นี่คือสามี
This is my husband.

sŏmchaay pen/khʉʉ khray?
สมชายคือใคร
Who is Somchai?

Note, however, that pen, not **khʉʉ**, is used in the contrastive construction **mây châ<u> </u> . . ., pen . . .** ('it's not . . ., it's . . .'):

mây châ<u> </u> yàaŋ nán, pen yàaŋ níi
ไม่ใช่อย่างนั้น เป็นอย่างนี้
It's not like that, it's like this.

mây châ<u> </u> fɛɛn pen nɔ́ɔŋ săaw
ไม่ใช่แฟน เป็นน้องสาว
She is not his girlfriend. She is his younger sister.

5.1.3 | mii

mii ('to have') is also used to translate 'there is/there are'; often, especially in written Thai, it occurs after the topic (9.1):

mii nák rian sìi rɔ́ɔy khon
มีนักเรียนสี่ร้อยคน
There are four hundred pupils.

mây mii weelaa
ไม่มีเวลา
There isn't time.

khon thay thîi phûut phaasăa faràŋsèet dâay dii mii nɔ́ɔy
คนไทยที่พูดภาษาฝรั่งเศสได้ดีมีน้อย
There are few Thais who can speak French well.
(people – Thai – who – speak – language – French – can – well – there – are – few)

5.1.4 yùu

yùu ('to be situated at') is used to describe the location of things:

bâan khun yùu thîi nǎy?
บ้านคุณอยู่ที่ไหน
Where is your house?

yùu nay tûu yen
อยู่ในตู้เย็น
It's in the fridge.

5.2 Stative verbs

Adjectives in Thai also function as stative verbs (verbs which describe a state rather than an action). Thus **lék** is both the adjective 'small' and the verb 'to be small':

bâan lék
บ้านเล็ก
a small house/The house is small.

sʉ̂a sǔay
เสื้อสวย
a pretty blouse/The blouse is pretty.

aahǎan phɛɛŋ
อาหารแพง
expensive food/The food is expensive.

Adjectives occur only rarely with the verb **pen** ('to be'); the following idiomatic expressions are exceptional:

pen hùaŋ	เป็นห่วง	to be concerned
pen sòot	เป็นโสด	to be single, unmarried
pen yày	เป็นใหญ่	to be in charge of

5.3 Verb compounds

Many verbs, such as **tèŋ ŋaan** ('to get married'), are made up of two words and are called verb compounds. Verb compounds in Thai can consist of (a) VERB + NOUN; (b) NOUN + VERB; or (c) VERB + VERB:

5.3.1 VERB + NOUN

khâw cay	เข้าใจ	to understand (to enter + heart)
dii cay	ดีใจ	to be happy (good + heart)
tèŋ ŋaan	แต่งงาน	to marry/be married (to arrange + work/party)
tham ŋaan	ทำงาน	to work (to do + work)

5.3.2 NOUN + VERB

cay dii	ใจดี	to be kind (heart + good)
cay yen	ใจเย็น	to be calm (heart + cool)
pàak ráay	ปากร้าย	to be malicious (mouth + bad)
hǔa khěŋ	หัวแข็ง	to be stubborn (head + hard)

5.3.3 VERB + VERB

plìan plɛɛŋ	เปลี่ยนแปลง	to change (change + change)
prìap thîap	เปรียบเทียบ	to compare (compare + compare)
òt yàak	อดอยาก	to be starving (go without + want)
duu lɛɛ	ดูแล	to look after (see + watch)
tòk loŋ	ตกลง	to agree (fall + descend)
dəən lên	เดินเล่น	to go for a walk (walk + play)
phûut lên	พูดเล่น	to joke (speak + play)

Verb compounds are negated by the pattern **mây** + VERB COMPOUND (11.1):

phǒm mây prìap thîap
ผมไม่เปรียบเทียบ
I'm not comparing.

5.4 Resultative verbs

A number of verbs, such as **nɔɔn làp** 'to sleep' (lie down + sleep) and **mɔɔŋ hěn** 'to see' (look at + see) resemble verb compounds as they consist of two verbs. They differ in that the second verb describes a state that results from the action of the first verb; thus, sleep results from lying down and seeing from looking. Verb compounds and verb + resultative verb constructions are negated differently (11.1, 11.2).

làp and **hěn** occur as resultative verbs only with **nɔɔn** and **mɔɔŋ** respectively. Other verbs have a much less restricted role as resultative verbs. These include the completive verbs, **sèt** ('to finish'), **còp** ('to complete'), **mòt** ('to be all used up/gone'), the directional verbs **khûn** ('to rise'), **loŋ** ('to descend'), **khâw** ('to enter') and **ɔ̀ɔk** ('to leave') (see 5.5), and words such as **than** ('to be in time') and **thùuk** ('to be correct, accurate'):

chán tham aahǎan sèt lέεw
ฉันทำอาหารเสร็จแล้ว
I've finished cooking.

kháw àan náŋsǔ̌ʉ còp lέεw
เขาอ่านหนังสือจบแล้ว
He's finished the book.

phǒm cháy ŋən mòt lέεw
ผมใช้เงินหมดแล้ว
I've spent all my money.

khun ca pay than máy?
คุณจะไปทันไหม
Will you get there in time?

Resultative verbs are negated by the pattern, VERB (PHRASE) + **mây** + RESULTATIVE VERB (11.2):

chán mɔɔŋ aray mây hěn
ฉันมองอะไรไม่เห็น
I can't see anything.

5.5   Directional verbs

The verbs **pay** ('to go') and **maa** ('to come') are used after a number of verbs or verb phrases as 'direction markers' to indicate whether the action of the verb is directed towards or away from the speaker. They commonly follow such verbs as **dəən** ('to walk'), **klàp** ('to return'), **yáay** ('to move home'), **thoo(rasàp)** ('to telephone'), **aw/phaa** ('to take'), **plìan** ('to change'), and **sòŋ** ('to send'). Some verbs conveying a sense of loss, such as **hǎay** ('to disappear') and **lɯɯm** ('to forget') occur only with **pay**:

raw yáay maa yùu kruŋthêep tâŋtɛ̀ɛ chán yaŋ dèk
เราย้ายมาอยู่กรุงเทพฯตั้งแต่ฉันยังเด็ก
We moved (here) to Bangkok when I was still a child.

wan sǎw nâa raw ca khàp rót pay hǔa hǐn
วันเสาร์หน้าเราจะขับรถไปหัวหิน
Next Saturday we'll drive to Hua Hin.

phrûŋ níi kháw ca aw náŋsɯ̌ɯ maa hây duu
พรุ่งนี้เขาจะเอาหนังสือมาให้ดู
Tomorrow he'll bring the book to show me.

khun ca phaa lûuk sǎaw pay dûay lǒɔ?
คุณจะพาลูกสาวไปด้วยหรือ
You're taking your daughter with you, then?

chán lɯɯm pay lɛ́ɛw
ฉันลืมไปแล้ว
I've forgotten.

mɯ̂a cháaw níi chán thoo(rasàp) pay khuy kàp phîi sǎaw
เมื่อเช้านี้ฉันโทร(ศัพท์)ไปคุยกับพี่สาว
I phoned your sister this morning.

Note, however, that in the expression, 'I'll ring you back', the directional verb is **maa**:

yen yen chán ca thoo(rasàp) maa mày
เย็น ๆ ฉันจะโทร(ศัพท์)มาใหม่
I'll ring you back in the evening.

pay and **maa** sometimes occur in the pattern VERB + **pay** + VERB + **maa**, where the same verb is repeated, to convey the idea of the action occurring repetitively back and forth:

phǒm dɔɔn pay dɔɔn maa sìp naathii
ผมเดินไปเดินมาสิบนาที
I walked back and forth for ten minutes.

raw khuy pay khuy maa tháŋ khɯɯn
เราคุยไปคุยมาทั้งคืน
We chatted (back and forth) all night long.

kháw chɔ̂ɔp plìan pay plìan maa
เขาชอบเปลี่ยนไปเปลี่ยนมา
He likes chopping and changing.

Other common directional verbs are **khûn** ('to rise'), **loŋ** ('to descend'), **khâw** ('to enter') and **ɔ̀ɔk** ('to leave'):

kháw piin khûn tônmáay
เขาปีนขึ้นต้นไม้
He climbed up the tree.

chán wîŋ loŋ banday
ฉันวิ่งลงบันได
I ran down the stairs.

raw dəən khâw hɔ̂ŋ
เราเดินเข้าห้อง
We entered the room.

kháw rîip ɔ̀ɔk pay
เขารีบออกไป
He hurried out.

In negative sentences directional verbs are not negated; note, however, that **khûn, loŋ, khâw** and **ɔ̀ɔk** also function as resultative verbs (11.2):

kháw yók mây khûn
เขายกไม่ขึ้น
He can't lift it.

chán kịn mây loŋ
ฉันกินไม่ลง
I can't eat it.

phǒm phûut mây ɔ̀ɔk
ผมพูดไม่ออก
I can't put it into words.

phǒm sày mây khâw
ผมใส่ไม่เข้า
I can't put it in.

5.6   Modal verbs

Modal verbs are auxiliary verbs which express such ideas as possibility, probability, ability, necessity, volition and obligation. Most Thai modal verbs can be followed by the particle **ca**; they are negated according to one of three different patterns (11.3).

5.6.1 Possibility and probability

The main modal verbs used for expressing possibility and probability are:

àat (ca)	อาจ(จะ)	may/might
khoŋ (ca)	คง(จะ)	will probably, sure to
yɔ̂m (ca)	ย่อม(จะ)	likely to
mák (ca)	มัก(จะ)	tends to, usually
hĕn (ca)	เห็น(จะ)	seems that

They all occur before the main verb and are negated by the pattern MODAL VERB (+ ca) + mây + VERB (PHRASE):

raw àat (ca) pay duu năŋ
เราอาจจะไปดูหนัง
We may go to see a film.

kháw khoŋ (ca) mây maa
เขาคง(จะ)ไม่มา
He probably won't come.

5.6.2 Ability and permission

The word 'can' can be translated by three Thai modal verbs – dâay, pen and wăy. All three verbs occur after the main verb and are negated by the pattern VERB (PHRASE) + mây + MODAL VERB.

5.6.2.1 VERB (PHRASE) + dâay

dâay conveys the sense of both ability and permission:

raw klàp maa phrûŋ níi dâay
เรากลับมาพรุ่งนี้ได้
We can come back tomorrow.

phŏm chûay kháw mây dâay
ผมช่วยเขาไม่ได้
I can't help her.

khɔ̌ɔ yɯɯm rót khun dâay máy?
ขอยืมรถคุณได้ไหม
Can I borrow your car?

The following idomatic expressions are also commonly used when talking about possibility:

pen pay dâay	เป็นไปได้	It's possible.
pen pay mây dâay	เป็นไปไม่ได้	It's impossible.
pen pay dâay máy?	เป็นไปได้ไหม	Is it possible?

Note that **dâay**, although written with a short vowel in Thai, is pronounced with a long vowel.

VERB (PHRASE) + **pen**

pen conveys the sense of knowing how to do something:

kháw phûut phaasǎa thay pen
เขาพูดภาษาไทยเป็น
He speaks/can speak Thai.

phǒm tham ̦aahǎan mây pen
ผมทำอาหารไม่เป็น
I can't cook.

khun khàp rót pen máy?
คุณขับรถเป็นไหม
Can you drive?

VERB (PHRASE) + **wǎy**

wǎy conveys the sense of being physically able to do something:

klay pay chán dəən mây wǎy
ไกลไป ฉันเดินไม่ไหว
It's too far. I can't walk.

rawaŋ nàk ná yók wǎy máy?
ระวังหนักนะ ยกไหวไหม
Be careful, it's heavy. Can you lift it?

Necessity: 'must' and 'need'

Necessity can be expressed by the following modal verbs which all occur before the main verb:

(ca) tôŋ	(จะ)ต้อง	must

tɔ̂ŋkaan (ca)	ต้องการ(จะ)	need
campen (ca)	จำเป็น(จะ)	necessary to
campen tɔ̂ŋ	จำเป็นต้อง	necessary to

tɔ̂ŋkaan (ca), campen (ca) and campen tɔ̂ŋ are negated by the pattern mây + MODAL VERB + VERB (PHRASE).

(ca) tɔ̂ŋ can be negated in two ways, but with different meanings: (a) (ca) mây tɔ̂ŋ + VERB (PHRASE) ('there is no need to . . .'); and (b) (ca) tɔ̂ŋ mây + VERB (PHRASE) ('must not . . .'):

khun tɔ̂ŋ chûay kháw nɔ̀y
คุณต้องช่วยเขาหน่อย
You must help him a bit.

raw tɔ̂ŋ mây lɯɯm
เราต้องไม่ลืม
We must not forget.

phǒm mây tɔ̂ŋ pay
ผมไม่ต้องไป
There's no need for me to go/I don't need to go.

mây tɔ̂ŋ lɔ̀k
ไม่ต้องหรอก
There's no need. (when declining an offer)

mây campen
ไม่จำเป็น
It's not necessary.

campen tɔ̂ŋ tham hây sèt wan níi
จำเป็นต้องทำให้เสร็จวันนี้
It's necessary to finish it today.

khun mây campen tɔ̂ŋ càay ŋən
คุณไม่จำเป็นต้องจ่ายเงิน
There's no need for you to pay any money.

5.6.4 | Obligation

Obligation is expressed by **khuan (ca)** ('should/ought') or **nâa (ca)** ('should/ought') before the main verb. Both are most commonly negated by the pattern **mây + MODAL VERB (+ ca) + VERB (PHRASE)**:

khun khuan ca bɔ̀ɔk phǒm lûaŋ nâa
คุณควรจะบอกผมล่วงหน้า
You should've told me in advance.

raw mây nâa ca klàp dὲk
เราไม่น่าจะกลับดึก
We ought not to return late.

5.6.5 *'want to'*

The idea of wanting to do something is expressed by **yàak (ca)** ('want to, would like to') which occurs before the main verb. Negative sentences follow the pattern **mây + yàak (ca) + VERB (PHRASE)**:

chán yàak (ca) klàp bâan
ฉันอยาก(จะ)กลับบ้าน
I'd like to go home.

kháw mây yàak khuy kàp phǒm
เขาไม่อยากคุยกับผม
She doesn't want to talk to me.

5.7 Time and aspect

Whether an action occurs in the future or the past (time), and whether it is a completed, continuous, or habitual action (aspect), can, when necessary, be clarified by using auxiliary verbs or particles.

5.7.1 *Future actions: ca + VERB (PHRASE)*

Actions that occur in the future can be described using the pattern **ca + VERB (PHRASE)**:

phrûŋ níi kháw ca mây maa
พรุ่งนี้เขาจะไม่มา
Tomorrow he won't come.

raw ca pay kɔ̀ samǔy
เราจะไปเกาะสมุย
We shall go to Koh Samui.

Completed actions: VERB (PHRASE) + lέεw
Attained states: STATIVE VERB + lέεw

Completed actions can be described by the pattern VERB (PHRASE) + lέεw ('already'):

kháw pay tham ŋaan lέεw
เขาไปทำงานแล้ว
He has gone to work.

raw kin khâaw lέεw
เรากินข้าวแล้ว
We have eaten already.

rót mee maa lέεw
รถเมล์มาแล้ว
The train has arrived/Here comes the train.

lέεw occurs with stative verbs to indicate that the specified state or condition has been attained:

thùuk lέεw
ถูกแล้ว
That's correct.

phɔɔ lέεw
พอแล้ว
That's enough.

dii lέεw
ดีแล้ว
That's fine.

Note that some non-stative verbs also occur with lέεw to convey the sense of a state being attained:

khâw cay lέεw
เข้าใจแล้ว
(Now) I understand.

fŏn tòk lέεw
ฝนตกแล้ว
It's (started) raining.

5.7.3 | *Continuous actions:* kamlaŋ + *VERB (PHRASE)* + yùu

Continuous actions, whether in the present or past, can be described by
the pattern kamlaŋ + VERB (PHRASE) + yùu:

chán kamlaŋ àan náŋsʉ̌ʉ yùu
ฉันกำลังอ่านหนังสืออยู่
I am/was reading.

Alternatively, either yùu or kamlaŋ may be dropped:

5.7.3.1 | kamlaŋ + VERB (PHRASE)

raw kamlaŋ kin khâaw
เรากำลังกินข้าว
We are/were eating.

5.7.3.2 | VERB (PHRASE) + yùu

kháw duu thii wii yùu
เขาดูทีวีอยู่
He is/was watching TV.

5.7.4 | *Actions about to happen:* kamlaŋ ca + *VERB (PHRASE)*

Actions about to happen, whether in the immediate future or when
narrating events in the past, are described by the pattern kamlaŋ ca +
VERB (PHRASE):

mɛ̂ɛ kamlaŋ ca triam aahǎan
แม่กำลังจะเตรียมอาหาร
Mum is/was about to prepare the food.

raw kamlaŋ ca kin khâaw
เรากำลังจะกินข้าว
We are/were about to eat.

phǒm kamlaŋ ca pay
ผมกำลังจะไป
I am/was about to go.

5.7.5 Actions that have just happened: phôŋ + VERB (PHRASE)

Actions that have just happened are described by the pattern phôŋ + VERB (PHRASE):

chán phôŋ sʉ́ʉ rót mày
ฉันเพิ่งซื้อรถใหม่
I have just bought a new car.

phŏm phôŋ hěn kháw
ผมเพิ่งเห็นเขา
I have just seen him.

kháw phôŋ rúu
เขาเพิ่งรู้
He has just found out/learned.

5.7.6 Single and habitual actions in the past: khəəy + VERB (PHRASE)

The pattern khəəy + VERB (PHRASE) is used to describe an action that (a) has occurred on at least one occasion in the past, or (b) that has occurred habitually in the past; it can occur with lέεw for added emphasis. When preceded by the negative word mây it means 'never' and often occurs in the pattern mây khəəy . . . maa kɔ̀ɔn ('never . . . before'):

chán khəəy pay thîaw chiaŋmày
ฉันเคยไปเที่ยวเชียงใหม่
I've been to Chiangmai.

phŏm khəəy duu lέεw
ผมเคยดูแล้ว
I've seen it already

raw khəəy yùu thîi kruŋthêep
เราเคยอยู่ที่กรุงเทพฯ
We used to live in Bangkok.

chán mây khəəy kin thurian
ฉันไม่เคยกินทุเรียน
I've never eaten durian.

phŏm mây khəəy hěn maa kɔ̀ɔn
ผมไม่เคยเห็นมาก่อน
I've never seen it before.

When **khəəy** occurs in questions, it means 'have you ever . . .?'; a 'yes'
answer is **khəəy**, a 'no' answer, **mây khəəy**:

khəəy pay thîaw phuukèt máy?
เคยไปเที่ยวภูเก็ตไหม
Have you ever been to Phuket?

khəəy/mây khəəy
เคย/ไม่เคย
Yes/No.

5.7.7 | Negative past tense: mây dây + VERB (PHRASE)

The pattern **mây dây** + VERB (PHRASE) is used to describe actions that
did not take place in the past; it cannot be used with stative verbs:

raw mây dây pay
เราไม่ได้ไป
We didn't go.

chán mây dây bɔɔk kháw
ฉันไม่ได้บอกเขา
I didn't tell him.

Note that it should not be assumed that the positive past tense is formed
by **dây** + VERB (PHRASE); this pattern occurs only rarely.

For other uses of **mây dây** + VERB (PHRASE), see 5.1.1, 11.4.

5.7.8 | past continuous tense: VERB (PHRASE) + maa + (dâay) + TIME EXPRESSION + lέεw

Actions that began in the past and continue through to the present can
be described by the pattern, VERB (PHRASE) + **maa** + (**dâay**) + TIME
EXPRESSION + **lέεw**:

raw nâŋ rót fay maa (dâay) sɔ̌ɔŋ chûamooŋ lέεw
เรานั่งรถไฟมา(ได้)สองชั่วโมงแล้ว
We have been sitting on the train for two hours.

kháw rian phaasǎa thay maa (dâay) lǎay pii lέεw
เขาเรียนภาษาไทยมา(ได้)หลายปีแล้ว
He has been studying Thai for many years.

For use of **dâay** to express duration of time, see Appendix 2.

5.7.9 | *Changed states: STATIVE VERB + khûn/loŋ*

The verbs **khûn** ('to ascend') and **loŋ** ('to descend') are used with pairs of contrasting stative verbs to indicate an increase or decrease in state; they are similar to English 'up' in 'heat up', 'speed up', etc. and 'down' in 'cool down', 'slow down', etc.

ûan khûn	อ้วนขึ้น	to get fatter	**phɔ̌ɔm loŋ**	ผอมลง	to slim down
rew khûn	เร็วขึ้น	to speed up	**cháa loŋ**	ช้าลง	to slow down
dii khûn	ดีขึ้น	to improve	**yɛ̂ɛ loŋ**	แย่ลง	to worsen
mâak khûn	มากขึ้น	to increase	**nɔ́y loŋ**	น้อยลง	to decrease

Note that **khûn** and **loŋ** also occur with verbs of motion as direction markers (5.5).

5.7.10 | *VERB (PHRASE) + wáy*

The verb **wáy** occurs after a verb of action, or verb phrase, to convey the idea that the action is being done for future use or reference:

chán ca kèp wáy kin phrûŋ níi
ฉันจะเก็บไว้กินพรุ่งนี้
I'll keep it to eat tomorrow.

fàak khɔ̌ɔŋ wáy thîi nîi dâay máy?
ฝากของไว้ที่นี่ได้ไหม
Can I leave my things here?

raw cɔɔŋ tǔa wáy lɛ́ɛw
เราจองตั๋วไว้แล้ว
We've booked tickets already.

kháw sɨ́ɨ wáy àan wan lǎŋ
เขาซื้อไว้อ่านวันหลัง
He bought it to read another day.

aw wáy wan lǎŋ
เอาไว้วันหลัง
Let's put it off to another day.

5.7.11 VERB (PHRASE) + aw

The verb **aw** occurs after a verb of action or verb phrase to convey the idea that the subject is doing something for himself; often **aw** is followed by **wáy**. The beginner is best advised to simply memorise examples from the speech of native speakers rather than to attempt to create sentences of their own using this pattern.

phǒm triam aw wáy lέεw
ผมเตรียมเอาไว้แล้ว
I've prepared things.

khun kèp aw wáy lέεw chây máy?
คุณเก็บเอาไว้แล้วใช่ไหม
You've kept it, right?

chán khít aw eeŋ
ฉันคิดเอาเอง
I thought so myself.

daw aw sí khá
เดาเอาซิคะ
Have a guess!

5.7.12 VERB (PHRASE) + sǐa/sá

sǐa, often shortened to **sá**, occurs widely after a verb phrase; it cannot be translated and is extremely difficult for the foreign learner to use correctly other than in pre-memorised expressions. One sense of **sǐa/sá** is 'too bad it happened that way':

kháw maa sǎay pay sá lέεw
เขามาสายไปเสียแล้ว
He came too late.

raw àat ca rúucàk kan dii kəən pay sá lέεw
เราอาจจะรู้จักกันดีเกินไปเสียแล้ว
Maybe we know each other too well.

kham wâa sǐa khâw cay yâak sá dûay
คำว่า เสีย เข้าใจยากเสียด้วย
The word **sǐa** is difficult to understand.

It also occurs in the pattern **mûarày ca** + VERB (PHRASE) + **sá thii**, to show irritation or impatience that something has not happened:

mûarày ca sèt sá thii?
เมื่อไรจะเสร็จเสียที
When are you going to be finished?

mûarày fŏn ca yùt tòk sá thii?
เมื่อไรฝนจะหยุดตกเสียที
When will it stop raining?

5.8 Passives

The passive construction is used much less commonly in Thai than in English. It is generally restricted to sentences with a negative connotation, where the subject is a victim of something unpleasant, such as being beaten, fined, robbed, arrested, criticised, gossiped about, cheated, attacked, shot, and so on. The passive is formed using the passive-marker **thùuk**, in the pattern SUBJECT + **thùuk** + (AGENT) + VERB (PHRASE):

chán thùuk yuŋ kàt
ฉันถูกยุงกัด
I've been bitten by a mosquito.

maalii thùuk rót chon
มาลีถูกรถชน
Malee was hit by a car.

kháw thùuk tamrùat càp
เขาถูกตำรวจจับ
He was arrested by a policeman.

raw thùuk khamooy
เราถูกขโมย
We were robbed.

phûan thùuk yiŋ taay
เพื่อนถูกยิงตาย
My friend was shot dead.

Much less common than **thùuk**, but used identically is the passive-marker **doon**:

kháw doon tii
เขาโดนตี
He was beaten.

74

English passive sentences that carry a neutral or positive connotation can often be rendered by the pattern SUBJECT + **dây ráp** ('received') + VERB (PHRASE):

raw dây ráp chəən pay . . .
เราได้รับเชิญไป . . .
We were invited to . . .

phǒm dây ráp anúyâat . . .
ผมได้รับอนุญาต . . .
I was permitted to . . .

kháw dây ráp lûak pen . . .
เขาได้รับเลือกเป็น . . .
He was chosen to be . . .

The pattern SUBJECT + **dây ráp** + NOUN is also commonly translated by the passive in English:

kháw dây ráp ìtthíphon càak . . .
เขาได้รับอิทธิพลจาก . . .
He was influenced by . . .

kháw dây ráp kaan sùksǎa càak ameerikaa
เขาได้รับการศึกษาจากอเมริกา
He was educated in America.

khɔ̂ɔ sanǒə dây ráp khwaam hěn chɔ̂ɔp
ข้อเสนอได้รับความเห็นชอบ
The proposal was approved.

English passive expressions like 'it is well known that . . .', 'it is generally accepted that . . .', and so on are formed using the pattern **pen thîi** + VERB + **kan** + **wâa . . .**:

pen thîi sâap kan dii wâa . . .
เป็นที่ทราบกันดีว่า . . .
It is well known that . . .

pen thîi yɔɔm ráp kan dooy thûa pay wâa . . .
เป็นที่ยอมรับกันโดยทั่วไปว่า . . .
It is generally accepted that . . .

5.9 Verbs of utterance, mental activity and perception with *wâa*

Verbs of utterance ('say, whisper, call', etc.), mental activity ('think, remember, hope', etc.) and perception ('see, understand, know', etc.) are followed by **wâa** + SUBORDINATE CLAUSE. **wâa** is similar in function to English 'that' (say that, think that, know that), but unlike 'that', which is optional in English, **wâa** should, at least in the early stages of learning, be regarded as compulsory:

khít wâa ca klàp phrûŋ níi
คิดว่าจะกลับพรุ่งนี้
I think (that) I'll return tomorrow.

wăŋ wâa ca mây phèt kəən pay
หวังว่าจะไม่เผ็ดเกินไป
I hope (that) it's not too spicy.

rúusʉ̀k wâa mây mɔ̀
รู้สึกว่าไม่เหมาะ
I feel (that) it's not appropriate.

Some of the most common verbs that are followed by **wâa** are:

bɔ̀ɔk	บอก	to say, tell
cam dâay	จำได้	to remember
chʉ̂a	เชื่อ	to believe
dây yin	ได้ยิน	to hear
hěn	เห็น	to see, think
klua	กลัว	to be afraid
khâw cay	เข้าใจ	to understand
khít	คิด	to think
nɛ̂ɛ cay	แน่ใจ	to be certain
pen hùaŋ	เป็นห่วง	to be concerned, worried
phûut	พูด	to say, speak
rúu	รู้	to know (facts) (informal)
rúusʉ̀k	รู้สึก	to feel

sâap	ทราบ	to know (facts) (formal)
sǒŋsǎy	สงสัย	to suspect
wǎŋ	หวัง	to hope

For further examples of the use of **wâa** see 9.3 and 12.4.

5.10 Verbs of emotion with *thîi*

Verbs of emotion ('to be angry, sorry, excited', etc.) are generally followed by **thîi** + SUBORDINATE CLAUSE. **thîi** is similar in function to English 'that' (sorry that, angry that, happy that), but unlike 'that', which is optional in English, **thîi** is compulsory:

phǒm sǐa cay thîi mây dây pay
ผมเสียใจที่ไม่ได้ไป
I'm sorry (that) I didn't go.

kháw kròot thîi chán súu
เขาโกรธที่ฉันซื้อ
He's angry (that) I bought it.

raw dii cay thîi nâa rɔ́ɔn phàan pay lέεw
เราดีใจที่หน้าร้อนผ่านไปแล้ว
We're pleased (that) the hot season is over.

5.11 Causatives

Causative constructions in Thai are formed using either (a) **tham** + VERB; (b) **hây** + VERB (PHRASE); or (c) **tham hây** + VERB (PHRASE). The nature of of the subject (whether it is human or non-human) and object (whether it is animate or inanimate), and the degree of intention, determine the appropriate construction.

5.11.1 SUBJECT (human or non-human) + **tham** + (inanimate OBJECT) + VERB

tham ('to make, do') combines with a number of verbs, such as **tòk** ('to fall') and **hǎay** ('to disappear') to express unintended causation:

kháw tham thûay tòk
เขาทำถ้วยตก
She dropped the cup.

chán tham nǎŋsǔ̀ hǎay
ฉันทำหนังสือหาย
I've lost the book.

Some common examples of verbs which occur in this pattern are:

tham . . . tòk (to fall)	ทำ . . . ตก	to drop something
tham . . . tɛ̀ɛk (to be broken)	ทำ . . . แตก	to break something
tham . . . pɯ̂an (to be dirty)	ทำ . . . เปื้อน	to make something dirty
tham . . . sǐa (to be spoiled)	ทำ . . . เสีย	to spoil something
tham . . . lòn (to fall)	ทำ . . . หล่น	to make something fall off
tham . . . lùt (to slip loose)	ทำ . . . หลุด	to let something slip
tham . . . hòk (to spill)	ทำ . . . หก	to spill something
tham . . . hàk (to break off)	ทำ . . . หัก	to make something break off

| 5.11.2 | SUBJECT (human) + **hây** + (animate OBJECT) + VERB (PHRASE) |

hây can convey a range of meanings, from the zero coercion of 'to let someone do something', to the more forceful 'to have someone do something' and 'to make someone do something':

mɛ̂ɛ hây phǒm rian banchii
แม่ให้ผมเรียนบัญชี
My mother had me study accountancy.

kháw hây chán klàp maa dɯan nâa
เขาให้ฉันกลับมาเดือนหน้า
They got me to come back next month.

phɔ̂ɔ hây lûuk pay dûay
พ่อให้ลูกไปด้วย
Father let his children go with him.

hây occurs as the first element in a number of common compound verbs which convey a sense of causation:

hây . . . duu (let/have + see)	ให้ . . . ดู	to show
hây . . . kɔ̀ɔt (let/have + happen)	ให้ . . . เกิด	to cause, create
hây . . . châw (let/have + rent)	ให้ . . . เช่า	to let
hây . . . yɯɯm (let/have + borrow)	ให้ . . . ยืม	to lend

hây kháw duu nɔ̀y
ให้เขาดูหน่อย
Show him/let him see.

raw hây phน̂an châw bâan raw
เราให้เพื่อนเช่าบ้านเรา
We let our house to a friend.

phǒm mây hây lûuk yน̄น̄m rót
ผมไม่ให้ลูกยืมรถ
I don't let my children borrow my car.

hây may be preceded by another verb specifying the method of causing someone to do something (e.g. by requesting, telling, ordering, etc.). Verbs which commonly precede **hây** include **bɔ̀ɔk** ('to tell'), **khɔ̌ɔ** ('to request'), **yɔɔm** ('to allow'), **anúyâat** ('to allow'), **sàŋ** ('to order'), **yàak** ('to want to') and **tน̄an** ('to warn'). Word order in such constructions is SUBJECT (human) + SPECIFYING VERB + **hây** + (animate OBJECT) + VERB (PHRASE):

phǒm bɔ̀ɔk hây kháw sน̄น̄
ผมบอกให้เขาซื้อ
I told him to buy it.

kháw khɔ̌ɔ hây chán pay ráp
เขาขอให้ฉันไปรับ
He asked me to go and collect him.

raw yàak hây khun klàp maa rew rew
เราอยากให้คุณกลับมาเร็ว ๆ
We want you to come back soon.

chán tน̄an hây khun maa kɔ̀ɔn weelaa
ฉันเตือนให้คุณมาก่อนเวลา
I warned you to come early.

Note, however, the order of object and **hây** can be reversed with the verbs **bɔ̀ɔk** ('to tell'), **khɔ̌ɔ** ('to request'), **anúyâat** ('to allow'), **sàŋ** ('to order') and **tน̄an** ('to warn'):

phǒm bɔ̀ɔk kháw hây sน̄น̄
ผมบอกเขาให้ซื้อ
I told him to buy it.

kháw khɔ̌ɔ chán hây pay ráp
เขาขอฉันให้ไปรับ
He asked me to go and collect him.

5.11.3 SUBJECT (human or non-human) + **tham**
hây + (OBJECT) + VERB (PHRASE)

This pattern conveys a sense of clear intention, co-ercion or non-accidental causation by the subject:

câw nâathîi tham hây phǒm sǐa weelaa mâak
เจ้าหน้าที่ทำให้ผมเสียเวลามาก
The official made me waste a lot of time.

aakàat ùn ùn tham hây kháw rúusɨk sabaay
อากาศอุ่น ๆ ทำให้เขารู้สึกสบาย
Warm weather makes her feel good.

trùat kaan bâan tham hây khruu pùat hǔa
ตรวจการบ้านทำให้ครูปวดหัว
Marking homework gives the teacher a headache.

For negative causatives, see 11.9.

5.12 'To give': direct and indirect objects

The order of objects with the verb **hây** ('to give') is SUBJECT + **hây** + DIRECT OBJECT (+ **kɛ̀ɛ**) + INDIRECT OBJECT. The preposition **kɛ̀ɛ** ('to, for') is frequently omitted, and in some instances, such as 'Have you fed the dog yet?', it must be omitted:

chán hây náŋsɨ̌ɨ (kɛ̀ɛ) kháw
ฉันให้หนังสือ(แก่)เขา
I gave him the book.

phɔ̂ɔ hây ŋən (kɛ̀ɛ) lûuk
พ่อให้เงิน(แก่)ลูก
The father gave his children money.

khun hây aahǎan mǎa rɨ́ yaŋ?
คุณให้อาหารหมาหรือยัง
Have you fed the dog yet? (you – give – food – dog – yet?)

If the direct object is quantified, the quantifier follows the indirect object:

chán hây náŋsɨ̌ɨ (kɛ̀ɛ) kháw sǎam lêm
ฉันให้หนังสือ(แก่)เขาสามเล่ม
I gave him three books.

If the direct object is qualified (e.g. by a relative clause), the qualifier follows the direct object, but the preposition kὲὲ becomes obligatory:

chán hây náŋsǔǔ thîi chán chɔ̂ɔp kὲὲ kháw
ฉันให้หนังสือที่ฉันชอบแก่เขา
I gave him books which I like.

phɔ̂ɔ hây ŋən hâa phan bàat nán kὲὲ lûuk
พ่อให้เงินห้าพันบาทนั้นแก่ลูก
The father gave his children the five thousand baht.

The indirect object (i.e. me) in sentences like 'he taught me Thai', 'she passed me the letter' and 'they brought me flowers' follows the pattern, VERB + DIRECT OBJECT + hây + INDIRECT OBJECT:

kháw sɔ̌ɔn phaasǎa thay hây phǒm
เขาสอนภาษาไทยให้ผม
He taught me Thai.

kháw sòŋ còtmǎay maa hây phǒm
เขาส่งจดหมายมาให้ผม
She passed me the letter.

kháw aw dɔ̀ɔkmáay maa hây phǒm
เขาเอาดอกไม้มาให้ผม
They brought me flowers.

5.13 Verb serialization

Verb serialization, in which a number of verbs sharing the same subject follow one after the other, with no intervening conjunctions or prepositions, is extremely common in Thai; and for beginners, learning to 'string' two or three verbs together comfortably is a key strategy in trying to reproduce authentic-sounding Thai. A random glance through examples in this book will show just how prevalent such patterns are.

Serial verb constructions can describe a sequence of consecutive actions:

kháw pay sɯ́ɯ maa kin
เขาไปซื้อมากิน
(he – go – buy – come – eat)
He went out to buy something and brought it back to eat.

Or a number of simultaneous actions:

kháw rîip wîŋ khâam pay

เขารีบวิ่งข้ามไป

(he – hurry – run – cross – go)

He hurriedly ran across.

Many learners understandably panic at the sight of a long string of verbs such as this, which seems at first sight to be an awesome serial verb construction:

tɔ̂ŋ rîip klàp pay rîak hây maa bɔ̀ɔk

ต้องรีบกลับไปเรียกให้มาบอก

must – hurry – return – go – summon – cause – come – tell

The problem in sentences like this is not so much the verbs that appear as the pronouns that have been omitted; once these are restored – or understood from the context – it becomes apparent that it is not one single serial verb construction and things become much more manageable:

(khun) tɔ̂ŋ rîip klàp pay rîak hây (kháw) maa bɔ̀ɔk (chán)

(คุณ)ต้องรีบกลับไปเรียกให้(เขา)มาบอก(ฉัน)

(you) – must – hurry – return – go – summon – cause – (him) – come – tell – (me)

You must hurry back and summon him to come and tell me.

Chapter 6

Adjectives (stative verbs) and adjectival constructions

As mentioned in the previous chapter, the categories 'verb' and 'adjective' overlap in Thai and many of the words that are considered to be adjectives in English are called stative verbs when describing Thai. For simplicity, however, the term 'adjective' is used throughout this chapter.

Adjectives do not occur with the verb **pen** ('to be') (5.1.1); they follow the noun they modify and in noun phrases they often occur with a classifier. The most common patterns of noun phrase in which an adjective occurs are listed in 3.5.6–3.5.10.

When a noun is modified by two adjectives (e.g. a large, red book) the normal word order in Thai is NOUN + ADJECTIVE + CLASSIFIER + ADJECTIVE:

náŋsɯ̌ɯ sǐi dɛɛŋ lêm yày
หนังสือสีแดงเล่มใหญ่
the large, red book (book – red – classifier – big)

sǎaw sǔay khon ruay
สาวสวยคนรวย
the beautiful, rich girl (girl – beautiful – classifier – rich)

mǎa kὲὲ tua sǐi dam
หมาแก่ตัวสีดำ
the old, black dog (dog – old – classifier – black)

In this pattern, the first adjective identifies the general category (red books, beautiful girls, old dogs) while the classifier + second adjective specifies the individual case.

6.1 Compound adjectives

As with nouns and verbs, compounding is a common way of creating new adjectives. The most productive adjectival prefixes are **cay** ('heart'), **nâa** ('worthy of') and **khîi** ('having the characteristic of'); of more limited usage are **châŋ** ('given to/good at') and **hǔa** ('head'). **cay** ('heart') also occurs as an adjectival suffix.

cay dii	ใจดี	kind (heart + good)
cay yen	ใจเย็น	calm (heart + cool)
cay rɔ́ɔn	ใจร้อน	impatient, impetuous (heart + hot)
cay khɛ̂ɛp	ใจแคบ	narrow-minded (heart + narrow)
nâa sǒn cay	น่าสนใจ	interesting (**sǒn cay** – to be interested in)
nâa bɨ̀a	น่าเบื่อ	boring (**bɨ̀a** – to be bored)
nâa lɨɨm	น่าลืม	forgettable (**lɨɨm** – to forget)
nâa klua	น่ากลัว	frightening (**klua** – to be afraid)
khîi kìat	ขี้เกียจ	lazy (**kìat** does not exist in isolation)
khîi aay	ขี้อาย	shy (**aay** – to be embarrassed)
khîi lɨɨm	ขี้ลืม	forgetful (**lɨɨm** – to forget)
khîi nǐaw	ขี้เหนียว	mean, stingy (**nǐaw** – to be sticky)
châŋ phûut	ช่างพูด	talkative (**phûut** – to speak)
châŋ khít	ช่างคิด	given to thinking (**khít** – to think)
châŋ sǎŋkèet	ช่างสังเกต	observant (**sǎŋkèet** – to observe)
châŋ thǐaŋ	ช่างเถียง	argumentative (**thǐaŋ** – to argue)
hǔa dii	หัวดี	clever (head + good)
hǔa khɛ̌ŋ	หัวแข็ง	stubborn, headstrong (head + hard)
hǔa sǔuŋ	หัวสูง	pretentious (head + high)
hǔa nɔ̂ɔk	หัวนอก	educated abroad (head + outside)
hǔa kàw	หัวเก่า	conservative, old-fashioned (head + old)

phɔɔ cay	พอใจ	satisfied (enough + heart)
klûm cay	กลุ้มใจ	depressed (gloomy + heart)
sabaay cay	สบายใจ	happy (well/happy + heart)
nàk cay	หนักใจ	worried (heavy + heart)

Another common stylistic feature of Thai is the use of two adjectives of identical or similar meaning. Common examples include:

kàw kɛ̀ɛ	เก่าแก่	old (old + old)
sǔay ŋaam	สวยงาม	beautiful (beautiful + beautiful)
wâaŋ plàaw	ว่างเปล่า	vacant, empty (vacant + empty)
yâak con	ยากจน	poor (difficult + poor)
yày too	ใหญ่โต	big (big + big)
yə́ yɛ́	เยอะเยะ	many (many + many)

6.2 Modification of adjectives

The meaning of adjectives can be modified by the addition of words such as 'not', 'very', 'rather', 'somewhat', and so on. A few adjectival modifiers occur before the adjective, while the majority occur after the adjective:

6.2.1 MODIFIER + ADJECTIVE

khɔ̂ɔn khâaŋ ca	ค่อนข้างจะ	rather
mây	ไม่	not
mây khɔ̂y ... thâwrày	ไม่ค่อย ... เท่าไร	not very

bâan mây khɔ̂y yày thâwrày
บ้านไม่ค่อยใหญ่เท่าไร
The house isn't very big.

6.2.2 ADJECTIVE + MODIFIER

ca taay	จะตาย	very (informal)
caŋ	จัง	really
ciŋ ciŋ	จริง ๆ	truly

dii	ดี	nice and . . .
kəən pay	เกินไป	too
kwàa	กว่า	more
khûn	ขึ้น	increasingly
loŋ	ลง	decreasingly
lŭa kəən	เหลือเกิน	excessively
mâak	มาก	very
mŭan kan	เหมือนกัน	fairly
nák	นัก	very
pay nɔ̀y	ไปหน่อย	a little bit too
phɔɔ	พอ	enough
phɔɔ cháy	พอใช้	enough
phɔɔ (phɔɔ) kan	พอ (ๆ) กัน	equally
phɔɔ sŏmkhuan	พอสมควร	enough
thâw (thâw) kan	เท่า (ๆ) กัน	equally
thii diaw	ทีเดียว	indeed
thîi sùt	ที่สุด	most

phaasăa phŏm mây dii phɔɔ
ภาษาผมไม่ดีพอ
My language isn't good enough.

Two modifiers can modify the same adjective:

khɔ̂ɔn khâaŋ ca phɛɛŋ pay nɔ̀y
ค่อนข้างจะแพงไปหน่อย
a little too much on the expensive side

hɔ̂ŋ níi ùn dii ciŋ ciŋ
ห้องนี้อุ่นดีจริง ๆ
This room is really nice and warm.

6.3 Special intensifiers

Certain adjectives are followed by specific intensifiers, which in the absence of a suitable equivalent in English (e.g. *brand* new, *pitch* black, *fast* asleep, etc.), can be translated as 'very'. Such intensifiers, used in moderation, can add a more lively flavour to descriptions and are a useful addition to the more advanced learner's vocabulary. Note that some adjectives (e.g. cold, red) have more than one specific intensifier, while some specific intensifiers can be used with more than one adjective.

6.3.1 General

asleep	làp + pǔy	หลับปุ๋ย
bewildered	ŋoŋ + ték	งงเต๊ก
big	yày + bə̂ə rə̂ə/ mahừ maa	ใหญ่เบ้อเร่อ/ มหึมา
bright	sawàaŋ + câa	สว่างจ้า
dark	mû̵ut + tút tûu	มืดตื๊ดตื๋อ
dull, insipid	cùut + chûut	จืดชืด
clear	sǎy + cɛ̌ɛw	ใสแจ๋ว
cold	yen + cíap/chìap	เย็นเจี๊ยบ/เฉียบ
correct	thùuk + pěŋ/pé	ถูกเป๋ง/เป๊ะ
crazy	bâa + chamát	บ้าชมัด
crowded	nɛ̂n + îat	แน่นเอี้ยด
different	tàaŋ kan + líp láp	ต่างกันลิบลับ
dry	hɛ̂ɛŋ + ŋɛ̌ɛ tɛ̌ɛ	แห้งแห้งแต่
equal	thâw kan + píap/pé	เท่ากันเปี๊ยบ/เป๊ะ
expensive	phɛɛŋ + líp lîw	แพงลิบลิ่ว
far	klay + líp lîw hàaŋ + líp lîw	ไกลลิบลิ่ว ห่างลิบลิ่ว
fat	ûan + pǐi	อ้วนปี๋
fast	rew + cǐi/prû̵u/rîi	เร็วจี๋/ปรื๋อ/รี่

flat	bɛɛn + tɛ́ɛt tɛ̆ɛ/tɛ̆ɛ	แบนแต๊ดแต่/แต่
frequent, in close succession	thìi + yíp	ถี่ยิบ
full	tem + ìat/prìi/prɛ̂ɛ	เต็มเอี้ยด/ปรี่/แปร้
full (food)	ìm + tʉ̂ʉ	อิ่มตื้อ
hard	khɛ̆ŋ + pǎŋ	แข็งปั๋ง
heavy	nàk + ʉ̂ŋ	หนักอึ้ง
hot	rɔ́ɔn + cǐi	ร้อนจี๋
humid, moist	chûm + chàm	ชุ่มฉ่ำ
identical	mʉ̆an kan + píap/pé	เหมือนกันเปี๊ยบ/เป๊ะ
lost	hǎay + tɔ́ɔm	หายต๋อม
loud	daŋ + prɛ̆ɛ/lân	ดังแปร๋/ลั่น
modern	than samǎy + cíap	ทันสมัยเจี๊ยบ
new	mày + ìam	ใหม่เอี่ยม
old	kàw + ŋâk	เก่างั้ก
pointed	lɛ̆ɛm + píap	แหลมเปี๊ยบ
round	klom + dìk	กลมดิก
sharp	khom + krìp	คมกริบ
silent	ŋîap + krìp	เงียบกริบ
similar	mʉ̆an + píap/pé mʉ̆an kan + dé/dík	เหมือนเปี๊ยบ/เป๊ะ เหมือนกันเด๊ะ/ดิ๊ก
skilful	khlɔ̂ŋ + prʉ̆ʉ	คล่องปรื๋อ
small	lék + kacít rít/ kacǐw rǐw/kacɔ́ɔy rɔ́ɔy	เล็กกะจิ๊ดริ๊ด/ กะจิ๋วริ๋ว/กะจ๋อยร๋อย
straight	troŋ + phɛ̆ŋ/pǎŋ/pé	ตรงแผง/เป๋ง/เป๊ะ
stupid	ŋôo + chamát	โง่ชะมัด
tall	sǔuŋ + príit sǔuŋ + líp lîw	สูงปรี๊ด สูงลิบลิ่ว
thick	nǎa + púk/tà	หนาปึ๊ก/เตอะ

tight	**kháp + pǔŋ**	คับปึ๋ง
urgent	**dùan + cǐi**	ด่วนจี๋

Colours

black	**dam + pǐi**	ดำปี๋
	dam + khlàp	ดำขลับ
green	**khǐaw + khacii**	เขียวขจี
	khǐaw + prɛ̌ɛ	เขียวแปร๋
	khǐaw + ʉ̌ʉ	เขียวอื๋อ
red	**dɛɛŋ + cɛ́ɛt**	แดงแจ๊ด
	dɛɛŋ + cɛ̌ɛ	แดงแจ๋
	dɛɛŋ + prɛ́ɛt	แดงแปร๊ด
white	**khǎaw + cúa**	ขาวจั๊วะ
	khǎaw + cúak	ขาวจวก
yellow	**lʉ̌aŋ + ɔ̌ɔy**	เหลืองออ๋ย
	lʉ̌aŋ + prɛ́ɛt	เหลืองแปร๊ด
	lʉ̌aŋ + cɔ̌ɔy	เหลืองจอย

Flavours

bitter	**khǒm + pǐi**	ขมปี๋
bland	**cʉ̀ʉt + chʉ̂ʉt**	จืดชืด
salty	**khem + pǐi**	เค็มปี๋
sour	**prîaw + cíit**	เปรี้ยวจี๊ด
spicy	**phèt + cǐi**	เผ็ดจี๋
sweet	**wǎan + cíap**	หวานเจี๊ยบ
	wǎan + cɔ̌ɔy	หวานจอย
	wǎan + chàm	หวานฉ่ำ

6.4 Reduplication

Reduplication (the repetition of a word, either in part or full) is another common means of modifying the meaning of adjectives in Thai. The two main forms of adjectival reduplication are simple repetition of the adjective and repetition of the adjective with tonal change.

6.4.1 Simple repetition of the adjective

One function of this type of reduplication is to make the meaning less precise, corresponding approximately to the adjectival suffix *-ish* in English:

sĭi dɛɛŋ dɛɛŋ	สีแดง ๆ	a reddish colour
bâan lék lék	บ้านเล็ก ๆ	a smallish house
aahǎan phèt phèt	อาหารเผ็ด ๆ	spicy-ish food

This type of reduplication sometimes indicates that the preceding noun is plural:

phûu yĭŋ sǔay sǔay	ผู้หญิงสวย ๆ	pretty girls
náŋsɨ̌ɨ dii dii	หนังสือดี ๆ	good books

6.4.2 Repetition of adjective with tonal change

The meaning of an adjective is intensified by reduplication when the first element is pronounced with an exaggerated high tone, regardless of the normal tone of the word; this exaggerated high tone is particularly apparent when reduplicating a word with a high tone like rɔ́ɔn ('hot') where the first element is pitched considerably higher and is usually accompanied by an exaggerated lengthening of the vowel. This type of reduplication tends to be a feature of female rather than male speech:

arɔ́y arɔ̀y	อร่อย อร่อย	Ever so tasty!
bɨ́a bɨ̀a	เบื่อ เบื่อ	So bored!
phɛ́ɛŋ phɛɛŋ	แพง แพง	Really expensive!

Sometimes the reduplication adds a third element, with the exaggerated high tone on the middle syllable:

dii díi dii	ดี ดี๊ ดี	So good!

6.5 Comparison of adjectives

The basic comparative construction employs the pattern ADJECTIVE + kwàa ('more than'):

khâaw nâa pèt arɔ̀y kwàa
ข้าวหน้าเป็ดอร่อยกว่า
Duck rice is tastier.

rót tooyootâa thùuk kwàa rót bens
รถโตโยต้าถูกกว่ารถเบนซ์
Toyotas are cheaper than Mercedes.

khâa khrûaŋ bin phɛɛŋ kwàa pii thîi lɛ́ɛw
ค่าเครื่องบินแพงกว่าปีที่แล้ว
The air fare is more expensive than last year.

câaŋ khon tham dii kwàa tham eeŋ
จ้างคนทำดีกว่าทำเอง
Paying someone to do it is better than doing it yourself.

6.5.1 Degrees of comparison

The basic comparative construction, ADJECTIVE + kwàa, can be modified by the addition of degree adverbs, such as mâak ('much, a lot'), yá ('much, a lot'), nítnɔ̀y ('a little'):

sanùk kwàa yá
สนุกกว่าเยอะ
a lot more fun

klay kwàa nítnɔ̀y
ไกลกว่านิดหน่อย
a little bit further

phɛɛŋ kwàa sɔ̌ɔŋ thâw
แพงกว่าสองเท่า
twice as expensive

| 6.5.2 | *Equal comparisons* |

| 6.5.2.1 | X + ADJECTIVE + **thâw kàp** ('as much as') + Y |

This is the most common pattern and is used both for numerically quantifiable and non-quantifiable comparisons:

lûuk sǔuŋ thâw kàp phɔ̂ɔ
ลูกสูงเท่ากับพ่อ
The son is as tall as his father.

nakhɔɔn phanom klay thâw kàp nɔ̌ɔŋkhaay
นครพนมไกลเท่ากับหนองคาย
Nakhorn Phanom is as far as Nongkhai.

pay rót fay thùuk thâw kàp pay rót mee
ไปรถไฟถูกเท่ากับไปรถเมล์
Going by train is as cheap as going by bus.

| 6.5.2.2 | X + **kàp** ('with') + Y + ADJECTIVE + **thâw (thâw) kan/ phɔɔ (phɔɔ) kan** ('equally') |

This pattern is a variation on 6.5.2.1:

phɔ̂ɔ kàp lûuk sǔuŋ thâw kan
พ่อกับลูกสูงเท่ากัน
Father and son are as tall as each other.

nakhɔɔn phanom kàp nɔ̌ɔŋkhaay klay thâw kan
นครพนมกับหนองคายไกลเท่ากัน
Nakhorn Phanom and Nongkhai are as far as one another.

pay rót fay kàp pay rót mee thùuk thâw kan
ไปรถไฟกับไปรถเมล์ถูกเท่ากัน
Going by train and going by bus are as cheap as each other.

| 6.5.2.3 | X + ADJECTIVE + **mǔan** ('similar') + Y |

Non-quantifiable adjectives can also occur in this pattern.

lûuk sǎaw sǔay mǔan mɛ̂ɛ
ลูกสาวสวยเหมือนแม่
The daughter is as beautiful as her mother.

aahǎan ciin arɔ̀y mǔan aahǎan thay
อาหารจีนอร่อยเหมือนอาหารไทย
Chinese food is as tasty as Thai food.

While the pattern X + kàp ('with') + Y + ADJECTIVE + mǔan kan is possible, it is ambiguous since . . . mǔan kan can mean 'fairly . . .' and is therefore best avoided:

mɛ̂ɛ kàp lûuk sǎaw sǔay mǔan kan
แม่กับลูกสาวสวยเหมือนกัน
Mother and daughter are as beautiful as each other.

or

Mother and daughter are fairly good looking.

6.5.2.4 X + ADJECTIVE + mây phɛ́ɛ ('not lose to') + Y

plaa prîaw wǎan arɔ̀y mây phɛ́ɛ kɛɛŋ kày
ปลาเปรี้ยวหวานอร่อยไม่แพ้แกงไก่
The sweet and sour fish is as tasty as the chicken curry.

lûuk sǎaw pàak ráay mây phɛ́ɛ mɛ̂ɛ
ลูกสาวปากร้ายไม่แพ้แม่
The daughter has as sharp a tongue as her mother.

6.5.3 *Interrogative comparisons*

Questions involving comparisons follow the pattern QUESTION WORD + ADJECTIVE + kwàa kan?:

thîi nǎy klay kwàa kan?
ที่ไหนไกลกว่ากัน
Which is further?

khray kèŋ kwàa kan?
ใครเก่งกว่ากัน
Who is the cleverer?

lêm nǎy thùuk kwàa kan?
เล่มไหนถูกกว่ากัน
Which book is cheaper?

6.5.4 | *Negative comparisons*

Basic negative comparison can be made by the pattern X + **sûu** + Y + **mây dâay** ('X can't beat Y'):

aahǎan faràŋ sûu aahǎan thay mây dâay
อาหารฝรั่งสู้อาหารไทยไม่ได้
Western food isn't as good as/can't beat Thai food.

More specific negative comparisons using adjectives (e.g. Western food is not as spicy as Thai food) are often reversed to produce a positive comparison (Thai food is spicier than Western food).

6.5.5 | *Excessives*

Excessive ('too . . .') constructions follow the pattern ADJECTIVE + (**kəən**) **pay** ('too much') with **kəən** frequently omitted, especially in conversational Thai:

klay (kəən) pay
ไกล(เกิน)ไป
It's too far.

rɔɔŋ tháaw kháp (kəən) pay
รองเท้าคับ(เกิน)ไป
The shoes are too tight.

This pattern, with **kəən** normally omitted, can be modified by the addition of the degree adverbs (7.6), **nɔ̀y** ('a little'), **nítnɔ̀y** ('a little bit') or **mâak** ('a lot'):

klay pay nɔ̀y
ไกลไปหน่อย
a little too far

cháa pay nítnɔ̀y
ช้าไปนิดหน่อย
a little bit too late

phɛɛŋ pay mâak*
แพงไปมาก
much too expensive

*In response to the question, **phɛɛŋ pay rɨ́ plàaw?** 'Is it too expensive?; as an initiating sentence, 'That's much too expensive', the normal word order would be **phɛɛŋ mâak pay.**

6.5.6 | *Superlatives*

Superlative constructions follow the pattern ADJECTIVE + **thîi sùt** ('most'):

thəə pen nák rɔ́ɔŋ daŋ thîi sùt khɔ̌ɔŋ thay
เธอเป็นนักร้องดังที่สุดของไทย
She is Thailand's most famous singer.

an nǎy thùuk thîi sùt?
อันไหนถูกที่สุด
Which is the cheapest one?

mây bɔ̀ɔk dii thîi sùt
ไม่บอกดีที่สุด
Best not to tell.

thîi sǎmkhan thîi sùt khɨɨ . . .
ที่สำคัญที่สุดคือ . . .
The most important thing is . . .

Chapter 7

Adverbs and adverbial constructions

7.1 Adverbs of manner

Adverbs of manner are indistinguishable in form from adjectives; thus **dii** means both 'good' and 'well' and **cháa** both 'slow' and 'slowly'.

For simplicity, the term 'adjective' is used in this chapter when describing the structure of adverbial phrases.

Verbs are modified according to the following main patterns:

1 VERB (PHRASE) + ADJECTIVE
2 VERB (PHRASE) + REDUPLICATED ADJECTIVE
3 VERB (PHRASE) + ADVERBIAL PHRASE
4 VERB (PHRASE) + **dây** + ADJECTIVE
5 VERB (PHRASE) + **hây** + ADJECTIVE

7.1.1 VERB (PHRASE) + ADJECTIVE

In the simplest adverbial constructions, the verb or verb phrase is followed by an adjective:

kháw dǝǝn cháa
เขาเดินช้า
He walks slowly.

khun phûut chát
คุณพูดชัด
You speak clearly.

khun khàp rót rew
คุณขับรถเร็ว
You drive quickly.

kháw càt hɔ̂ŋ sǔay
เขาจัดห้องสวย
She arranged the room nicely.

7.1.2 | VERB (PHRASE) + REDUPLICATED ADJECTIVE

As noted in the previous chapter (6.4), reduplication often moderates the meaning of an adjective:

kháw sɯ́ɯ thùuk thùuk
เขาซื้อถูก ๆ
He bought cheap(ish)ly.

kháw dəən cháa cháa
เขาเดินช้า ๆ
He walks slow(ish)ly.

chán ca pay rew rew níi
ฉันจะไปเร็ว ๆ นี้
I'm going shortly.

Reduplication is also commonly used in commands, either with or without **hây** (see 7.1.5); commands can be made more polite by the addition of **nɔ̀y** at the end:

maa rew rew
มาเร็ว ๆ
Come quickly!

yùu ŋîap ŋîap
อยู่เงียบ ๆ
Stay quiet!

phûut daŋ daŋ nɔ̀y
พูดดัง ๆ หน่อย
Speak up!

Sometimes, however, it is difficult to distinguish any real difference in meaning between a single and reduplicated form; in cases where the reduplicated form is preferred, it seems to be because it creates a rhythm that is more pleasing to the ear:

chán klìat ciŋ ciŋ
ฉันเกลียดจริง ๆ
I really hate him.

yùu klây klây
อยู่ไกล้ ๆ
It's nearby.

Reduplication, sometimes with a different vowel in the second syllable, is also used as an onomatopoeic device, to imitate, for example, sounds of laughter, rain and animal cries:

kháw hǔa rɔ́ khík khík
เขาหัวเราะคิกๆ
She giggled.

mɛɛw rɔ́ɔŋ míaw míaw
แมวร้องเมี๊ยว ๆ
The cat miaowed.

fǒn tòk sǐaŋ pɔ̀ pὲ
ฝนตกเสียงเปาะแปะ
The rain pitter-pattered.

7.1.3   VERB (PHRASE) + ADVERBIAL PHRASE

Another common way of forming adverbial constructions involves the use of 'adverb formers' of which the most common are **yàaŋ** ('like, as'), **dooy** ('by'), **dûay** ('with') and **pen** ('is, as'); **yàaŋ** is followed by a verb or verb phrase, **dooy** by a verb or noun phrase, and **dûay** and **pen** by a noun phrase:

7.1.3.1   VERB (PHRASE) + **yàaŋ** + VERB (PHRASE)

kháw phûut yàaŋ mây suphâap
เขาพูดอย่างไม่สุภาพ
He spoke impolitely.

kháw yím yàaŋ mii khwaam sùk
เขายิ้มอย่างมีความสุข
She smiled happily.

7.1.3.2   VERB (PHRASE) + **dooy** + VERB PHRASE

kháw phûut dooy mây khít kɔ̀ɔn
เขาพูดโดยไม่คิดก่อน
He spoke without thinking.

kháw yɔɔm ráp kham wicaan dâay dooy ŋâay
เขายอมรับคำวิจารณ์ได้โดยง่าย
He could accept the criticism readily/easily.

kháw tham dooy mây wăŋ phŏn tɔ̀ɔp thɛɛn
เขาทำโดยไม่หวังผลตอบแทน
He did it without hope of anything in return.

raw tham eeŋ dâay dooy mây tôŋ phɨ̂ŋ khon ɨ̀ɨn
เราทำเองได้โดยไม่ต้องพึ่งคนอื่น
We can do it ourselves without having to depend on other people.

For examples of VERB (PHRASE) + **dooy** + NOUN PHRASE, see 8.4.

7.1.3.3 | VERB (PHRASE) + **dûay** + NOUN PHRASE

kháw tham ŋaan dûay khwaam yâak lambàak
เขาทำงานด้วยความยากลำบาก
He worked with difficulty.

For further examples, see 8.4.

7.1.3.4 | VERB (PHRASE) + **pen** + NOUN PHRASE

kháw càay ŋən pen wan wan
เขาจ่ายเงินเป็นวัน ๆ
They pay daily.

kháw bɛ̀ɛŋ pen chín lék lék
เขาแบ่งเป็นชิ้นเล็ก ๆ
She divided it into small pieces.

7.1.4 | **VERB (PHRASE) + dâay + ADJECTIVE**

When describing how well someone can do something, the adjective
follows the auxiliary verb **dâay**:

kháw phûut dâay khlɔ̂ŋ
เขาพูดได้คล่อง
He speaks fluently.

khun khĭan dâay sŭay
คุณเขียนได้สวย
You write nicely.

mɛ̂ɛ tham aahǎan dâay arɔ̀y
แม่ทำอาหารได้อร่อย
Mum is a good cook. ('cooks food tastily')

VERB (PHRASE) + hây + ADJECTIVE

When giving commands as to how someone should do something, the
causative verb **hây** can be used before the adjective:

kin hây mòt
กินให้หมด
Eat everything up!

tham hây sèt
ทำให้เสร็จ
Finish it off!

tɛ̀ŋ tua hây rîaprɔ́ɔy
แต่งตัวให้เรียบร้อย
Dress respectably!

khǐan hây dii
เขียนให้ดี
Write nicely!

7.2 Modification of adverbs

Adverbs are modified in the same way as adjectives (see 6.2). A small
number of modifiers occur in the pattern VERB (PHRASE) + MODIFIER +
ADJECTIVE:

phǒm rian mây kèŋ
ผมเรียนไม่เก่ง
I don't do well in my studies.

kháw phûut mây khɔ̂y chát
เขาพูดไม่ค่อยชัด
He doesn't speak very clearly.

tham aahǎan khɔ̂ɔn khâaŋ ca sanùk
ทำอาหารค่อนข้างจะสนุก
Cooking is quite fun.

Other adverbial modifiers follow the pattern VERB (PHRASE) + ADJEC-TIVE + MODIFIER:

khun phûut rew mâak
คุณพูดเร็วมาก
You speak very quickly.

kháw tèŋ tua rîapróoy khûn
เขาแต่งตัวเรียบร้อยขึ้น
He dresses more respectably.

7.3 Comparison of adverbs

The comparison of adverbs follows the same pattern as that of adjectives (6.5), but with a verb preceding the adjective.

The basic comparative form is VERB (PHRASE) + ADJECTIVE + **kwàa**:

khun tham aahăan ารòy kwàa chán
คุณทำอาหารอร่อยกว่าฉัน
You are a better cook than me. (you – make food – more tasty than – me)

kháw phûut thay dâay chát kwàa phŏm
เขาพูดไทยได้ชัดกว่าผม
He speaks Thai more clearly than me.

7.3.1 Equal comparisons can be expressed as follows.

7.3.1.1 X + VERB (PHRASE) + ADJECTIVE + **thâw kàp** + Y

chán rian nàk thâw kàp phîi
ฉันเรียนหนักเท่ากับพี่
I study as hard as my sister.

7.3.1.2 X + **kàp** + Y + VERB (PHRASE) + ADJECTIVE + **thâw (thâw) kan/phɔɔ (phɔɔ) kan**

chán kàp phîi rian nàk thâw (thâw) kan
ฉันกับพี่เรียนหนักเท่า (ๆ) กัน
I and my sister study as hard as each another.

7.3.1.3 X + VERB (PHRASE) + ADJECTIVE + **mŭan** + Y

lûuk săaw tὲŋ tua sŭay mŭan daaraa năŋ
ลูกสาวแต่งตัวสวยเหมือนดาราหนัง
Her daughter dresses as beautifully as a film star.

7.3.2 The excessive construction is VERB
(PHRASE) + ADJECTIVE + (**kəən**) **pay**:

khun phûut rew (kəən) pay
คุณพูดเร็ว(เกิน)ไป
You speak too quickly.

7.3.3 The superlative construction is VERB
(PHRASE) + ADJECTIVE + **thîi sùt**:

thəə rɔ́ɔŋ phrɔ́ thîi sùt
เธอร้องเพราะที่สุด
She is the best singer.

7.3.4 *'As . . . as possible'*

The 'as . . . as possible' construction can be expressed in two ways, the
first involving the repetition of the adjective and the second using the
verb **tham** ('to do') instead of the repeated adjective.

7.3.4.1 VERB (PHRASE) + **yàaŋ** + ADJECTIVE + **thîi sùt** + **(thâw)**
thîi ca + ADJECTIVE + **dâay**

kháw wîŋ yàaŋ rew thîi sùt (thâw) thîi ca rew dây
เขาวิ่งอย่างเร็วที่สุด(เท่า)ที่จะเร็วได้
He ran as quickly as possible.

7.3.4.2 VERB (PHRASE) + **yàaŋ** + ADJECTIVE + **thîi sùt** + **(thâw) thîi**
ca + **tham** + **dâay**

phŏm ca tham yàaŋ dii thîi sùt (thâw) thîi ca tham dâay
ผมจะทำอย่างดีที่สุด(เท่า)ที่จะทำได้
I shall do it as well as possible.

7.4 Adverbs of time

Since verbs do not indicate tense in Thai, adverbs and adverbials (adverb phrases) are essential to specify when events take place.

Common adverbials of time include:

Present:	**dǐaw níi** (เดี๋ยวนี้)	now, at this moment	
	tɔɔn níi (ตอนนี้)	now	
	pàtcuban níi (ปัจจุบันนี้)	nowadays	
	thúk wan níi (ทุกวันนี้)	these days	
Past:	**mûa kɔ̀ɔn** (เมื่อก่อน)	before, formerly	
	tɔɔn nán (ตอนนั้น)	at that time	
	mûa kîi níi (เมื่อกี้นี้)	a minute ago	
Future:	**phrûŋ níi** (พรุ่งนี้)	tomorrow	
	wan lǎŋ (วันหลัง)	another day, some other day	
	khráŋ nâa (ครั้งหน้า)	next time	

These adverbial phrases can occur either before or after the verb phrase:

tɔɔn níi kháw mây wâaŋ
ตอนนี้เขาไม่ว่าง
He is not free at the moment.

mûa kɔ̀ɔn chán mây chɔ̂ɔp
เมื่อก่อนฉันไม่ชอบ
Before, I did not like it.

phǒm pay yîam wan lǎŋ
ผมไปเยี่ยมวันหลัง
I'll go to visit her another day.

A more extensive list of time expressions appears in 14.7.

Two important adverbs of time which do have a fixed position are **yaŋ** ('still') and **lέεw** ('already'). **yaŋ** occurs immediately before the verb or verb phrase and **lέεw** immediately after:

chán yaŋ hǐw
ฉันยังหิว
I'm still hungry.

kháw pay lέεw
เขาไปแล้ว
He's already gone.

7.5   Adverbs of frequency

The following adverbs of frequency occur only after a verb or verb phrase:

bɔ̀y bɔ̀y	บ่อย ๆ	often
samɤ̌ɤ	เสมอ	always
rɥ̂ay rɥ̂ay	เรื่อย ๆ	continuously
pen pracam	เป็นประจำ	regularly
pen rayá rayá	เป็นระยะ ๆ	periodically

raw pay thîaw mɥaŋ thay bɔ̀y bɔ̀y
เราไปเที่ยวเมืองไทยบ่อย ๆ
We visit Thailand often.

kháw tham aahǎan phèt samɤ̌ɤ
เขาทำอาหารเผ็ดเสมอ
She always makes spicy food.

chán pay hǎa mɔ̌ɔ pen rayá rayá
ฉันไปหาหมอเป็นระยะ ๆ
I go to see the doctor periodically.

The words **thammadaa** ('normally, usually') and **pòkkati** ('normally, usually') both occur more commonly at the beginning of a clause or sentence:

thammadaa phǒm mây kin lâw
ธรรมดาผมไม่กินเหล้า
Normally I don't drink alcohol.

pòkkati mii khon mâak
ปกติมีคนมาก
Usually there are a lot of people.

Other expressions of frequency, such as **baaŋ khráŋ** ('sometimes'), **thúk wan** ('daily'), **aathít la sɔ̌ɔŋ khráŋ** ('twice a week'), can occur either before the subject of a sentence or at the end of a sentence:

baaŋ khráŋ chán rúusɛ̀k bɛ̀a
บางครั้งฉันรู้สึกเบื่อ
Sometimes I feel bored.

chán rúusɛ̀k bɛ̀a baaŋ khráŋ
ฉันรู้สึกเบื่อบางครั้ง
I feel bored sometimes.

7.6 Adverbs of degree

The following adverbs of degree occur only after a verb or verb phrase:

mâak	มาก	a lot, very much, really
bâaŋ	บ้าง	somewhat
mɛ̌an kan	เหมือนกัน	somewhat; fairly/reasonably
nítnɔ̀y	นิดหน่อย	a little (bit)
nɔ̀y	หน่อย	a little

kháw maw mâak
เขาเมามาก
He's really drunk.

chán hǐw nítnɔ̀y
ฉันหิวนิดหน่อย
I'm a bit hungry.

thon nɔ̀y ná
ทนหน่อยนะ
Be a little patient!

mɛ̌an kan is widely used to express qualified or polite agreement or enthu-
siasm – although this usage is curiously ignored in most dictionaries. It
commonly occurs in the pattern **kɔ̂ɔ ...** + VERB (PHRASE) + **mɛ̌an kan**
when a negative response would be tactless:

aacaaŋ sɔ̌ɔn dii máy?
อาจารย์สอนดีไหม
Is he a good teacher?

– kɔ̂ɔ ... dii mɛ̌an kan
– ก็ ... ดีเหมือนกัน
– Well ... yes.

While **mâak** and **nítnɔ̀y** also occur as quantifiers (13.12), it is important to distinguish between the adverb **bâaŋ** and the similar-sounding quantifier, **baaŋ**; the fact that both are often glossed as 'some' in dictionaries is a common source of confusion for the learner.

As a quantifier, **baaŋ** ('some') is always followed by a classifier, although it is not always preceded by a noun:

chán chɔ̂ɔp kin aahǎan khɛ̀ɛk baaŋ yàaŋ
ฉันชอบกินอาหารแขกบางอย่าง
I like some kinds of Indian food.

baaŋ khon dii baaŋ khon mây dii
บางคนดี บางคนไม่ดี
Some people are good, some are bad.

bâaŋ normally modifies a verb and conveys the sense of 'to some extent' or 'somewhat'; it also occurs with Wh- questions, where it anticipates a plural answer (12.2.13). **bâaŋ** never occurs with classifiers:

kháw phûut phaasǎa thay dâay bâaŋ
เขาพูดภาษาไทยได้บ้าง
He speaks some Thai.

phǒm lên dâay bâaŋ
ผมเล่นได้บ้าง
I can play a bit/somewhat.

chán yàak pay kin aahǎan khɛ̀ɛk bâaŋ
ฉันอยากไปกินอาหารแขกบ้าง
I'd like to eat some Indian food.

kháw phûut ciŋ bâaŋ mây ciŋ bâaŋ
เขาพูดจริงบ้าง ไม่จริงบ้าง
(he – speak – true – somewhat, not – true – somewhat)
Some of what he says is true, some isn't.

hàt phûut khwaam ciŋ bâaŋ sí
หัดพูดความจริงบ้างซิ
(practise – speak – truth – somewhat – *command particle*)
Try telling the truth!

khun phóp kàp khray bâaŋ?
คุณพบกับใครบ้าง
Who did you meet?

One curious usage of **bâaŋ** is in the expression **bâaŋ kɔ̂ ... bâaŋ kɔ̂ ...**
('some ... and some ...'), which is identical in meaning to **baaŋ khon**:

bâaŋ kɔ̂ dii bâaŋ kɔ̂ mây dii
บ้างก็ดี บ้างก็ไม่ดี
Some people are good, some are bad.

bâaŋ kɔ̂ chɔ̂ɔp bâaŋ kɔ̂ mây chɔ̂ɔp
บ้างก็ชอบ บ้างก็ไม่ชอบ
Some like it, some don't.

Chapter 8

Location markers and other prepositions

An important function of prepositions is to indicate location. This chapter introduces the major location markers and then looks at a few of the different ways of dealing with the English prepositions 'to', 'for', 'by', 'with' and 'from'.

8.1 Location: *thîi* and *yùu*

The most basic location words are formed using the preposition **thîi** ('at') followed by the demonstratives, **nîi**, **nân** or **nôon**:

thîi nîi	ที่นี่	here
thîi nân	ที่นั่น	there
thîi nôon	ที่โน่น	over there

In a simple sentence stating the location of something, **thîi** follows the verb **yùu** ('to be situated at'):

yùu thîi nîi
อยู่ที่นี่
Here it is/It's here.

bâan yùu thîi nôon
บ้านอยู่ที่โน่น
The house is over there.

thîi is optional after the verb **yùu**, and frequently omitted:

chán yùu mɯaŋ thay naan
ฉันอยู่เมืองไทยนาน
I have lived in Thailand a long time.

kháw yùu bâan tɔɔn yen
เขาอยู่บ้านตอนเย็น
He is at home in the evenings.

| 8.1.1 | **khâŋ + PREPOSITION** |

The following prepositions can all be prefixed by **khâŋ** ('side'):

nay	ใน	in
nɔ̂ɔk	นอก	outside of
bon	บน	on, on top of; upstairs
lâaŋ	ล่าง	underneath; downstairs
nâa	หน้า	in front of
lăŋ	หลัง	behind
khâaŋ	ข้าง	by the side of

However, when a noun or noun phrase follows the preposition, **khâŋ** is usually dropped:

yùu nay rót
อยู่ในรถ
It's in the car.

yùu lăŋ bâan
อยู่หลังบ้าน
It's behind the house.

But if no noun follows the preposition, **khâŋ** cannot be dropped:

yùu khâŋ nɔ̂ɔk
อยู่ข้างนอก
It's outside.

yùu khâŋ bon
อยู่ข้างบน
It's on top/upstairs.

Note that as a prefix **khâŋ** is written with a long vowel symbol but pronounced with a short vowel.

8.1.2 phaay + PREPOSITION

Several of the prepositions above (8.1.1) can be prefixed by **phaay** ('side, part'):

phaay nay	ภายใน	within, internal
phaay nɔ̀ɔk	ภายนอก	outside, external
phaay tâay	ภายใต้	under, inferior position
phaay nâa	ภายหน้า	ahead, in the future
phaay lăŋ	ภายหลัง	afterwards, later on

phaay nay cèt wan
ภายในเจ็ดวัน
within seven days

phaay tâay ìtthíphon khɔ̌ɔŋ kháw
ภายใต้อิทธิพลของเขา
under his influence

8.1.3 thaaŋ + right/left

thaaŋ ('way') prefixes the words for **sáay** ('left') and **khwǎa** ('right') when describing locations; **mɯɯ** ('hand') may optionally be added to the end of the phrase:

yùu thaaŋ khwǎa
อยู่ทางขวา
It's on the right.

yùu thaaŋ sáay mɯɯ
อยู่ทางซ้ายมือ
It's on the left-hand side.

8.1.4 Non-prefixed prepositions

Common location prepositions which do not take any prefix include:

rawàaŋ	ระหว่าง	between
klay	ไกล	far
klây	ใกล้	near

troŋ khâam	ตรงข้าม	opposite
rim	ริม	on the edge of
taam	ตาม	along

8.2 'To'

Neither motion towards a place (I went to Thailand), nor indirect object with 'to give' (see 5.12) require prepositions in Thai; speaking *to* someone, uses the preposition kàp ('with'):

phǒm dəən thaaŋ pay mɯaŋ thay
ผมเดินทางไปเมืองไทย
I travelled to Thailand.

kháw hây náŋsɯ̌ɯ chán
เขาให้หนังสือฉัน
He gave the book to me.

chán yàak ca phûut kàp kháw
ฉันอยากจะพูดกับเขา
I'd like to speak to him.

8.3 'For'

The Thai words most commonly used to translate 'for' are hây, phɯ̂a, sǎmràp and sùan. While the distinctions are sometimes elusive and there is some overlap in usage, some broad principles can be applied.

8.3.1.1 hây

hây is used to express the idea of doing something for somebody, or getting someone to do something for you:

phǒm sɯ́ɯ náŋsɯ̌ɯ hây khun
ผมซื้อหนังสือให้คุณ
I bought a book for you.

phǒm ca bɔ̀ɔk (kháw) hây (khun)
ผมจะบอก(เขา)ให้(คุณ)
I'll tell him for you.

chûay pìt pratuu hây (chán) nɔ̀y
ช่วยปิดประตูให้(ฉัน)หน่อย
Please shut the door for me.

8.3.1.2 | phûa

phûa can be translated as 'for the sake of' and often conveys an idea of altruism or self-sacrifice. Note also, low-tone phùa which is used when inviting someone to do something on one's behalf in expressions like 'Have one (e.g. a beer) for me':

thúk sìŋ thúk yàaŋ phǒm tham phûa khun
ทุกสิ่งทุกอย่างผมทำเพื่อคุณ
Everything I do is for you.

chán tham ŋaan phûa anaakhót khɔ̌ɔŋ raw
ฉันทำงานเพื่ออนาคตของเรา
I am working for our future.

kháw sǐa salà tua phûa prathêet châat
เขาเสียสละตัวเพื่อประเทศชาติ
He sacrificed himself for the nation.

raw sɯ́ɯ aahǎan phûa bɔɔrícàak
เราซื้ออาหารเพื่อบริจาค
We bought food for donating.

kin phùa dûay ná
กินเผื่อด้วยนะ
Eat some for me, too, OK?

8.3.1.3 | sǎmràp

sǎmràp means both 'for' and, at the beginning of a sentence, 'as for', 'as far as . . . is concerned':

nîi sǎmràp khun
นี่สำหรับคุณ
This is for you.

sǎmràp aahǎan yen raw ca pay kin khâŋ nɔ̂ɔk
สำหรับอาหารเย็นเราจะไปกินข้างนอก
As far as the evening meal is concerned, we will eat out.

8.3.1.4 | sùan

sùan also means 'as for' and is used to introduce a statement:

sùan phǒm khít wâa mây dii ləəy
ส่วนผม คิดว่าไม่ดีเลย
As for me, I don't think it is good at all.

Two other common uses of 'for' in English are to express duration of time (I have studied Thai *for* three years) and to give reasons (I am angry with him *for* gossiping about me). Duration of time requires no preposition in Thai (14.7.5); reason clauses are introduced by **thîi**:

phǒm rian phaasǎa thay sǎam pii lɛ́ɛw
ผมเรียนภาษาไทยสามปีแล้ว
I have studied Thai for three years.

raw pay sɔ̌ɔŋ wan thâwnán
เราไปสองวันเท่านั้น
We are only going for three days.

chán kròot kháw thîi (kháw) ninthaa chán
ฉันโกรธเขาที่(เขา)นินทาฉัน
I am angry with him for gossiping about me.

khɔ̌ɔthôot thîi phǒm maa cháa
ขอโทษที่ผมมาช้า
I am sorry that I'm late.

8.4 'By'

The two Thai words most commonly used to translate 'by' are **dooy** and **dûay**; both are used to indicate the means of doing something:

chán pay dooy rót mee*
ฉันไปโดยรถเมล์
I went by bus.

raw bin pay mʉaŋ thai dooy sǎay kaan bin thay
เราบินไปเมืองไทยโดยสายการบินไทย
We flew to Thailand by Thai Airways.

khun tham dûay/dooy wíthii nǎy
คุณทำด้วย/โดยวิธีไหน
How did you do it? (you – do – by – method – which?)

khun tham dûay mʉʉ lɔ̌ɔ?
คุณทำด้วยมือหรือ
You did it by hand, then?

*Note, however, that while **dooy** can be used with all means of transportation, in practice it is commonly avoided. Instead, travelling somewhere as a passenger in a vehicle is expressed by the pattern **nâŋ** ('to sit') + VEHICLE + **pay/maa** + PLACE:

chán nâŋ rót mee pay chiaŋmày
ฉันนั่งรถเมล์ไปเชียงใหม่
I went to Chiangmai by bus.

To indicate that someone drove the vehicle, **nâŋ** is replaced by an appropriate verb meaning 'to drive' – **khàp** (for cars), **khìi** (for motorcycles, horses, bicycles) or **thìip** (for pedal trishaws):

phǒm khàp rót maa
ฉันขับรถมา
I came by car (as the driver)/I drove here.

raw khìi mɔɔtəəsay pay hǔa hǐn
เราขี่มอเตอร์ไซค์ไปหัวหิน
We went to Hua Hin by motorcycle/We motorcycled to Hua Hin.

'By' in English is also used to indicate (i) the agent in a passive sentence (He was hit *by* a car: 5.8); (ii) place (It is *by* the television); and (iii) time limitation (I must finish *by* Friday). As a location word, 'by' can be translated as **klây klây** ('near') or **khâŋ khâaŋ** ('next to, beside'); time limit can be conveyed by **kɔɔn** ('before') or **phaay nay** ('within'):

yùu klây klây/khâŋ khâaŋ thii wii
อยู่ใกล้ ๆ /ข้าง ๆ ทีวี
It is by the TV.

chán tɔ̂ŋ tham hây sèt kɔɔn/phaay nay wan sùk
ฉันต้องทำให้เสร็จก่อน/ภายในวันศุกร์
I have to finish it by Friday.

8.5 'With'

'With' in English is used mainly to indicate (i) accompaniment (I went *with* a friend) and (ii) instrument (She hit her husband *with* a stick). Accompaniment, in Thai, is conveyed by **kàp**:

chán pay kàp phɨ̂an
ฉันไปกับเพื่อน
I went with a friend.

Instrument is less clear-cut. **dûay** can be used in the pattern SUBJECT + VERB (PHRASE) + **dûay** + INSTRUMENT, but it often sounds unnatural; instead, many native speakers favour the pattern SUBJECT + **cháy** (to use) + INSTRUMENT + VERB (PHRASE):

thəə cháy máy tii phǔa

เธอใช้ไม้ตีผัว

She hit her husband with a stick/She used a stick to hit . . .

raw tɔ̂ŋ cháy mɯɯ kin

เราต้องใช้มือกิน

We shall have to eat with our hands.

And **kàp** is also sometimes used to indicate instrument in the expressions **hěn kàp taa** ('to see with one's own eyes') and **faŋ kàp hǔu** ('to hear with one's own ears').

8.6 'From'

'From' can most frequently be translated by **càak**:

kháw maa càak chiaŋmày

เขามาจากเชียงใหม่

He comes from Chiangmai.

chán dây còtmǎay càak mɛ̂ɛ

ฉันได้จดหมายจากแม่

I got a letter from my mother.

raw nâŋ rót mee càak hǔa hǐn pay kruŋthêep

เรานั่งรถเมล์จากหัวหินไปกรุงเทพฯ

We went from Hua Hin to Bangkok by bus.

When 'from' identifies the beginning of a period of time, **tâŋtɛ̀ɛ** ('since') is used, either in the pattern **tâŋtɛ̀ɛ** + TIME WORD + **thǔŋ** ('till') + TIME WORD, or **tâŋtɛ̀ɛ** + TIME WORD + **maa**:

tâŋtɛ̀ɛ cháaw thǔŋ yen

ตั้งแต่เช้าถึงเย็น

from morning till evening

tâŋtɛ̀ɛ pii sɔ̌ɔŋ phan hâa rɔ́ɔy sìi sìp maa

ตั้งแต่ปี ๒๕๔๐ มา

from the year 2540/since 2540

tâŋtɛ̀ɛ wan nán maa

ตั้งแต่วันนั้นมา

from that day

Chapter 9

Clauses and sentences

9.1 Word order and topicalisation

Word order in a sentence generally follows the pattern SUBJECT + VERB + OBJECT:

subject	verb	object
phɔɔ	**sɯɯ**	**rót**
พ่อ	ซื้อ	รถ
Father	bought	a car
chán	**rák**	**khun**
ฉัน	รัก	คุณ
I	love	you

In spoken Thai it is common for the subject noun to be followed immediately by its pronoun; the beginner needs to be alert to distinguish this noun-pronoun apposition from similar-looking possessive phrases (3.5.12):

phɔɔ kháw sɯɯ rót
พ่อเขาซื้อรถ
(father – he – buy – car)
Father bought a car.

khruu kháw mây maa
ครูเขาไม่มา
(teacher – he – not – come)
The teacher didn't come.

rót man tìt
รถมันติด
(cars – they – stuck)
The traffic is jammed.

However, either subject or object, or even both, may be omitted when they are understood from the context. In the following sentence, for example, neither subject, direct object nor indirect object are stated, leaving just a 'string' of four verbs (5.13):

tɔ̂ŋ rîip pay sɯ́ɯ hây
ต้องรีบไปซื้อให้
(must – hurry – go – buy – give)
I must rush off and buy some for her.

Another common pattern, known as topicalisation, involves placing a word or phrase other than the subject at the beginning of the sentence, so that it becomes the 'topic' of the sentence (i.e. what the sentence is 'about').

sɯ̂a kàw ca aw pay bɔricàak phrûŋ níi
เสื้อเก่าจะเอาไปบริจาคพรุ่งนี้
(clothes – old – will – take – donate – tomorrow)
I'll give away the old clothes tomorrow.

aahǎan thîi lɯ̌a raw ca kin phrûŋ níi
อาหารที่เหลือเราจะกินพรุ่งนี้
(food – which – remains – we – will – eat – tomorrow)
We'll eat the food that is left over tomorrow.

faràŋ thîi tèŋ ŋaan kàp khon thay dǐaw níi mii yə́
ฝรั่งที่แต่งงานกับคนไทยเดี๋ยวนี้มีเยอะ
(Westerners – who – marry – with – Thais – now – there are – many)
Now there are lots of Westerners who are married to Thais.

phûuyǐŋ khon nán (phǒm) khít wâa pen khon yîipùn
ผู้หญิงคนนั้น(ผม)คิดว่าเป็นคนญี่ปุ่น
(girl – classifier – that – (I) – think – that – is – person – Japanese)
I think that girl is Japanese.

In spoken Thai, the particle **nâ/nâa** is often used at the end of the topic phrase (10.3.1.5).

In written Thai, the topic is often introduced by **sùan** ('as for'), **sǎmràp** ('as for') or **rûaŋ** ('about, concerning'); the end of a long topic clause is often marked by **nán** and the verb in the following clause introduced by **kɔ̂** ('so, therefore, well, then'):

sùan ahǎan kaan kin kàp thîi phák kɔ̂ cháy dâay
ส่วนอาหารการกินกับที่พักก็ใช้ได้
As for the food and accommodation, it was alright.
(as for – food – eating – with – place to stay – well, then – acceptable)

náŋsŭʉ thîi phǒm àan yùu nán nâa bʉ̀a ciŋ ciŋ
หนังสือที่ผมอ่านอยู่นั้นน่าเบื่อจริง ๆ
The book I'm reading is really boring.

9.2 Subordinate clauses

Subordinate clauses frequently occur before the main clause. Some subordinate and main clauses are linked by paired conjunctions, one at the beginning of each clause. **kɔ̂** (see 9.1), although often optional, is used extensively in introducing the main clause. Some common examples of paired conjunctions are:

thâa (hàak wâa) . . . kɔ̂ . . .	if . . . then . . . (9.2.1)
kaan thîi . . . kɔ̂ . . .	the fact that . . ., so . . . (9.2.2)
thʉ̌ŋ mɛ́ɛ wâa . . . tὲɛ . . .	although . . ., but . . . (9.2.3)
nɔ̂ɔk càak (nán lɛ́ɛw) . . . yaŋ . . .	apart from (that) . . ., still . . . (9.2.5)
phɔɔ . . . púp . . .	no sooner . . . than . . . (9.2.6)
. . . púp . . . páp	no sooner . . . than . . . (9.2.6)

9.2.1 | *Conditional clauses: 'if'*

Conditional sentences can be formed by the pattern, **thâa ... kɔ̂ + VERB**
('If ... then ...'); alternative words for 'if' are **thâa hàak wâa, hàak wâa,
hàak tὲὲ wâa**:

thâa hàak wâa fǒn tòk chán kɔ̂ (ca) mây pay
ถ้าหากว่าฝนตกฉันก็(จะ)ไม่ไป
If it rains, I'm not going/If it had rained, I wouldn't have gone, etc.

Often, however, the 'if' word is omitted, and in abrupt speech, even **kɔ̂**,
too:

fǒn tòk (kɔ̂) mây pay
ฝนตก(ก็)ไม่ไป
If it rains, I'm not going/If it had rained, I wouldn't have gone, etc.

The conditional clause and main clause may be linked by **lá kɔ̂** (or **lá
kɔ̂ɔ**, with a lengthened vowel on the second syllable), in which case the
verb normally follows:

(thâa khun) mây rîip lá kɔ̂ɔ mây than
(ถ้าคุณ)ไม่รีบละก็ไม่ทัน
If you don't hurry, you won't be in time.

9.2.2 | *Reason clauses: 'the fact that/because'*

Reason clauses commonly involve the expression, **kaan thîi** ('the fact
that'), which can be used in two patterns.

9.2.2.1 | **kaan thîi ... kɔ̂ + phrɔ́ wâa ...** ('The fact that ... is because ...')

In this pattern, the consequence is stated first and the reason or cause
given in the second clause:

kaan thîi phǒm klàp dὺk kɔ̂ phrɔ́ wâa pay thîaw kàp phɯ̂an
การที่ผมกลับดึกก็เพราะว่าไปเที่ยวกับเพื่อน
The fact that I'm home late is because I went out with friends.

kaan thîi kháw mây yɔɔm bin pay kɔ̂ phrɔ́ wâa kháw klua
การที่เขาไม่ยอมบินไปก็เพราะว่าเขากลัว
The fact that he won't agree to fly is because he is scared.

9.2.2.2 **kaan thîi . . . kôɔ + VERB** ('the fact that/because . . . so . . .')

In this pattern, the reason or cause is stated in the first clause and the consequence or conclusion follows in the second:

kaan thîi fǒn tòk nàk raw kôɔ maa cháa nɔ̀y
การที่ฝนตกหนักเราก็มาช้าหน่อย
Because it was raining heavily, we were a bit late.

kaan thîi kháw kin mòt kôɔ mây dây mǎay khwaam wâa arɔ̀y
การที่เขากินหมดก็ไม่ได้หมายความว่าอร่อย
The fact that he ate it all doesn't mean it tasted good.

In both patterns it is not unusual for **kaan** to be dropped and the sentence to begin with **thîi**:

thîi phǒm phûut yàaŋ nán kôɔ phrɔ́ wâa kròot
ที่ผมพูดอย่างนั้นก็เพราะว่าโกรธ
The fact that I spoke like that was because I was angry.

thîi kháw yaŋ mây klàp maa chán kôɔ tɔ̂ŋ rɔɔ
ที่เขายังไม่กลับมาฉันก็ต้องรอ
Because he hasn't come back yet, I shall have to wait.

'Owing/due to . . .' sentences, follow a similar pattern but are prefaced by **nûaŋ càak**, or the rather more formal-sounding **nûaŋ (maa) càak kaan thîi . . .** ('owing to the fact . . .'):

nûaŋ càak rót tìt mâak kháw kôɔ khoŋ maa cháa
เนื่องจากรถติดมากเขาก็คงมาช้า
Due to the heavy traffic jams, he will probably be late.

In written Thai **cɯŋ** is commonly used instead of **kôɔ**:

kaan thîi yaŋ mây mii khàaw cɯŋ mây sǎamâat bɔ̀ɔk dâay
การที่ยังไม่มีข่าวจึงไม่สามารถบอกได้
Because there is still no news, it is therefore impossible to say.

9.2.3 *Concessive clauses: 'although'*

Concessive clauses concede or admit a fact and begin with either **(thǔŋ) mέε wâa** ('although') or **tháŋ tháŋ thîi** ('although'); the main clause counters or contradicts that fact and frequently begins with **tὲε (kôɔ)** ('but'):

(thɤ̆ŋ) mɛ́ɛ wâa chán sày nám plaa yɤ́ tɛ̀ɛ (kɔ̂) yaŋ mây arɔ̀y
(ถึง)แม้ว่าฉันใส่น้ำปลาเยอะแต่(ก็)ยังไม่อร่อย
Although I put a lot of fish sauce in, it still doesn't taste good.

(thɤ̆ŋ) mɛ́ɛ wâa phǒm rák kháw tɛ̀ɛ kháw (kɔ̂) mây rák phǒm
(ถึง)แม้ว่าผมรักเขาแต่เขา(ก็)ไม่รักผม
Although I love her, she doesn't love me.

tháŋ tháŋ thîi fǒn tòk tɛ̀ɛ raw (kɔ̂) yaŋ pay
ทั้ง ๆ ที่ฝนตกแต่เราก็ยังไป
Although it's raining, we're still going.

Another kind of concessive clause is formed by the pattern, **mây wâa ca** ('regardless, no matter') + VERB + QUESTION WORD; the main clause may be introduced by **kɔ̂**:

mây wâa ca phɛɛŋ khɛ̂ɛ nǎy kɔ̂ yaŋ rúusɤ̀k khúm
ไม่ว่าจะแพงแค่ไหนก็ยังรู้สึกคุ้ม
Regardless of how expensive it was, I still think it was worth it.

mây wâa ca dəən pay nǎy kɔ̂ ca hěn tɛ̀ɛ khon nâa bɤ̂ŋ
ไม่ว่าจะเดินไปไหนก็จะเห็นแต่คนหน้าบึ้ง
No matter where you walk, you see only people with sullen faces.

mây wâa ca bɔ̀ɔk kìi khráŋ kháw kɔ̂ khoŋ mây yɔɔm faŋ
ไม่ว่าจะบอกกี่ครั้งเขาก็คงไม่ยอมฟัง
No matter how many times you tell him, he won't listen.

9.2.4 | *Purpose clauses: 'in order to'*

Purpose clauses often begin with **phɤ̂a (thîi) ca** ('in order to'):

kháw kin aahǎan thùuk thùuk phɤ̂a (thîi) ca prayàt ŋən
เขากินอาหารถูก ๆ เพื่อ(ที่)จะประหยัดเงิน
He eats cheap food in order to economise.

phǒm tham yàaŋ nán phɤ̂a (thîi) ca chûay phɤ̂an
ผมทำอย่างนั้นเพื่อ(ที่)จะช่วยเพื่อน
I did that in order to help a friend.

raw ca dəən thaaŋ klaaŋ khɤɤn phɤ̂a ca dây mây sǐa weelaa
เราจะเดินทางกลางคืนเพื่อจะได้ไม่เสียเวลา
We'll travel overnight so as not to waste time.

Additive clauses: 'apart from'

A common pattern for giving additional information is nɔ̂ɔk càak ...
lέɛw ... yaŋ ... (dûay) ('apart from ... still ... (too)'):

nɔ̂ɔk càak chiaŋmày lέɛw raw yaŋ pay thîaw lampaaŋ dûay
นอกจากเชียงใหม่แล้ว เรายังไปเที่ยวลำปางด้วย
Apart from Chiangmai, we went to Lampang, too.

nɔ̂ɔk càak ca kin nám man yə́ lέɛw khâa sɔ̂ɔm yaŋ phɛɛŋ dûay
นอกจากจะกินน้ำมันเยอะแล้ว ค่าซ่อมยังแพงด้วย
Apart from using a lot of petrol, the repair costs are expensive, too.

nɔ̂ɔk càak nán lέɛw yaŋ mii săahèet ìik lăay yàaŋ
นอกจากนั้นแล้ว ยังมีสาเหตุอีกหลายอย่าง
Apart from that, there are many other reasons.

9.2.6 **Time clauses**

Some common time clause expressions include:

phɔɔ ... púp (kɔ̂) ...	พอ ... ปุ๊บ(ก็) ...	no sooner ... than ...
... púp .... páp	... ปุ๊บ ... ปั๊บ	no sooner ... than ...
mûa ... (kɔ̂)	เมื่อ ... (ก็) ...	when (past) ...
weelaa ... (kɔ̂)	เวลา ... (ก็) ...	when ...
lăŋ càak thîi ... (kɔ̂)	หลังจากที่ ... (ก็) ...	after ...
kɔ̀ɔn thîi ... (kɔ̂)	ก่อนที่ ... (ก็) ...	before ...
khanà thîi ... (kɔ̂)	ขณะที่ ... (ก็) ...	while ...
tɔɔn thîi ... (kɔ̂)	ตอนที่ ... (ก็) ...	while ...
nay rawàaŋ thîi ... (kɔ̂)	ในระหว่างที่ ... (ก็) ...	while ...

phɔɔ nâŋ loŋ nâa thii wii púp kɔ̂ làp
พอนั่งลงหน้าทีวีปุ๊บก็หลับ
No sooner does he sit down in front of the TV than he falls asleep.

kin púp ìm páp
กินปุ๊บอิ่มปั๊บ
No sooner do I (start to) eat than I feel full.

mûa rian náŋsǔǔ phǒm kɔ̂ sùup burìi yǝ́

เมื่อเรียนหนังสือผมก็สูบบุหรี่เยอะ

When I was a student, I smoked a lot.

kɔ̀ɔn thîi ca thɔ̌ɔn ŋǝn chán kɔ̂ tôŋ prùksǎa kàp fɛɛn

ก่อนที่จะถอนเงินฉันก็ต้องปรึกษากับแฟน

Before withdrawing the money, I'll have to discuss it with my husband.

khanà thîi phǒm khuy thoorasàp yùu kɔ̂ mii khon maa rîak

ขณะที่ผมคุยโทรศัพท์อยู่ก็มีคนมาเรียก

While I was chatting on the phone, someone called me.

Direct and indirect speech

Both direct and indirect speech are introduced by **wâa** (5.9). When pronouns are omitted in the second clause, direct and indirect speech become identical in form. **wâa** plays the role of inverted commas in direct speech and 'that' in indirect speech:

kháw bɔ̀ɔk wâa (kháw) ca mây pay

เขาบอกว่า(เขา)จะไม่ไป

He said that he's not going.

kháw bɔ̀ɔk wâa (phǒm) ca mây pay

เขาบอกว่า(ผม)จะไม่ไป

He said, 'I'm not going.'

For indirect questions, see 12.4.

Imperatives

A simple verb or verb phrase is the most basic form of command. This can sound abrupt and is normally softened by adding the mild command particle **sí** or **thǝ̀** at the end of the sentence, or the more insistent particle **sîi** (10.3). Commands can be further softened by the use of polite particles (10.1):

duu sí

ดูซิ

Look!

pìt pratuu sí khá

ปิดประตูซิคะ

Shut the door, please.

Commands can also be expressed by the patterns VERB (PHRASE) + REDUPLICATED ADJECTIVE (7.1.2) and VERB + **hây** + ADJECTIVE (7.1.5):

phûut dii dii
พูดดี ๆ
Speak nicely!

càt hây rîapróoy
จัดให้เรียบร้อย
Arrange things tidily!

First person imperatives ('Let's . . .') can be expressed by the pattern, VERB (PHRASE) + **thəə**:

pay kin khâŋ nɔ̀ɔk thəə
ไปกินข้างนอกเถอะ
Let's go and eat out!

coŋ is an imperative which appears in written instructions, as for example, at the top of an examination paper:

coŋ tɔ̀ɔp kham thǎam
จงตอบคำถาม
Answer the (following) questions.

See also negative imperatives (11.8) and requesting someone to do/not do something (15.4.4, 15.4.5).

9.5 Exemplification

Examples are commonly enclosed within the 'wrap-around' pattern **chên . . . pen tôn** ('for example, . . .'); however, either **chên** or **pen tôn** may be omitted:

tɔ̂ŋ tham lǎay yàaŋ chên sák phâa hǔŋ khâaw tàt yâa pen tôn
ต้องทำหลายอย่างเช่นซักผ้า หุงข้าว ตัดหญ้าเป็นต้น
I have to do lots of things, such as washing, cooking and cutting the grass.

'To give an example' is **yók** ('to raise') **tua yàaŋ** ('example'):

khɔ̌ɔ yók tua yàaŋ nɘ̀ŋ
ขอยกตัวอย่างหนึ่ง
Let me give an example.

9.6 Exclamatory particles

âaw	อ้าว	Contradicting, chiding; disappointment: *Hey!*; *Oh!* (Is that so?).
é	เอ๊ะ	Surprise: *Eh?*; *What?*
ée	เอ๊	Thinking or wondering: *Ermm . . .*
hôəy	เฮ้ย	Calling attention: *Hey! Hold on a minute!*
mɛ̌ɛ	แหม	Surprise: *Goodness!*
ôo hoo	โอ้โฮ	Surprise: indignation; *Wow! Oh yeah?*
ɔ̂ɔ	อ้อ	Realization: *Ah!* (Now I understand).
táay	ต๊าย	Shock, horror: *Good Lord!* More common in female speech; variations include **táay taay**, **taay lɛ́ɛw** and **taay ciŋ**.
úy	อุ๊ย	Pain or mishap: *Ouch!*; *Oops!*

Chapter 10

Sentence particles

Sentence particles occur at the end of an utterance and serve a grammatical or communicative function. They can be divided into three main groups: (a) question particles; (b) polite particles; and (c) mood particles.

10.1 Question particles

Question particles are relatively straightforward. They are few in number and all occur at the end of an utterance to transform it into a question which requires a 'yes/no' answer. They are dealt with in 12.1.

10.2 Polite particles

Polite particles are added to the end of an utterance to show respect to the addressee. The most common are **khráp**, used by males at the end of statements and questions, **khâ** used by females at the end of statements and **khá**, also used by females, but at the end of questions:

pay nǎy khráp?
ไปไหนครับ
Where are you going? (male asking)

– **klàp bâan khâ**
– กลับบ้านค่ะ
– I'm going home. (female responding)

arɔ̀y máy khá?
อร่อยไหมคะ
Is it tasty? (female asking)

– **arɔ̀y khráp**
– อร่อยครับ
– Yes. (male responding)

Polite particles are also used as response particles to mean 'yes' or, when preceded by the negative particle **mây**, 'no'.

Polite particles are used after someone's name to call their attention; the female particles **khá** and **cá** are sometimes pronounced **khǎa** and **cǎa** respectively, the change of tone and vowel-lengthening signalling the speaker's closeness or desired closeness to the person she is addressing.

> **khun̩ mɛ̂ɛ khǎa?**
> คุณแม่ขา
> Mummy? (daughter speaking)
> – **cǎa**
> – จ๋า
> – Yes? (mother responding)

The most common polite particles are as follows.

10.2.1   khráp (ครับ)

Used by male speakers only, at the end of both statements and questions as a sign of politeness; used after a name to attract that person's attention; used in isolation as a response when one's name is called (when the vowel is often lengthened to **khráap**); used in isolation as a 'yes' response (12.1.2; 12.1.4); used, often repetitively, to reassure speaker of one's attention, for example on the telephone (**khráp ... khráp ... khráp**); used after **mây** to mean 'no'. In Bangkok speech the **r** is typically lost and **khráp** becomes **kháp**.

10.2.2   khráp phǒm (ครับผม)

Used by male speakers only; interchangeable with **khráp** (above) except it is not used in isolation with the negative **mây**; usage has only become widespread in the last decade or so, and may be just a passing fad. Often used humorously as a sign of exaggerated deference or politeness.

10.2.3   khá (คะ)

Used by female speakers only, at the end of questions as a sign of politeness; used after a name to attract that person's attention; used in isolation as a response when one's name is called; used in polite requests after the particle **sí**.

10.2.4   khâ (ค่ะ)

Used by female speakers only, at the end of statements as a sign of polite-ness; used in isolation as a response when one's name is called (when the vowel is often lengthened to khâa); used in isolation as a 'yes' response (12.1.2; 12.1.4); used to reassure speaker of one's attention (khâ . . . khâ . . . khâ) when the vowel may also be lengthened to khâa; used after mây to mean 'no'.

10.2.5   khǎa (ขา)

Used by female speakers only after a name to attract the person's atten-tion; can also be used in isolation as a response when one's name is called.

10.2.6   há?/há (ฮะ)

Used by male speakers as an informal substitute for khráp; used by female speakers as an informal substitute for khá; male pronunciation is charac-terised by a distinctive final glottal stop not associated with female usage.

10.2.7   hâ (ฮ่ะ)

Used by female speakers as an informal substitute for khâ.

10.2.8   cá (จ๊ะ)

Used by adult male and female speakers at the end of questions when talking to children, servants or people of markedly lower social status; used as a 'sweet-talk' question particle between males and females or as a 'best friends' question particle between females; used after the name of a child, servant or inferior to attract that person's attention; used in polite requests after the particle sí.

10.2.9   câ (จ๊ะ)

Used by adult male and female speakers at the end of a statement when speaking to children, servants and people of inferior status; between males and females denotes anything from easy familiarity to 'sweet talk'; between females signals 'best friends talk'; used as a response when one's name is called (when the vowel is often lengthened to câa); used in isolation as a 'yes' response; used to reassure speaker of one's attention (câa . . .

câa ... câa) when the vowel is normally lengthened; used after **mây** to mean 'no'.

10.2.10 căa (จ๋า)

Used by older or senior male and female speakers after a younger or junior person's name to attract that person's attention (e.g. parents or adults calling children); similarly used between equals as a sign of affection; can also be used in isolation as a response, more typically by females, when one's name is called.

10.2.11 wá/wâ/wóoy (วะ/ว่ะ/โว้ย)

An impolite or informal particle, used to indicate rudeness, anger and aggressiveness when speaking to strangers, or intimacy with close friends of equal status; **wá** is used with questions and **wâ/wóoy** with statements; more common in male speech but can be used by females; it is the particle favoured by baddies on the big screen, used by drinking friends as the evening progresses, and the one to snarl in the expression **tham aray wá?** ('What the hell are you doing?') if you have the misfortune to encounter an intruder in your house.

10.2.12 yá/yâ (ยะ/ย่ะ)

An impolite or informal particle, similar to **wá/wâ** (above), but restricted in usage to female speakers.

10.2.13 phâyâkhâ (พะยะค่ะ)/pheekhá (เพคะ)

When speaking to royalty, male speakers use **phâyâkhâ** and female speakers **pheekhá**.

10.3 Mood particles

Mood particles represent a major obstacle for the serious learner. Their function is often conveyed in English purely by intonation, so they cannot easily be translated; to complicate matters, one particle may have several variant forms, involving a change in tone or vowel length, with each form reflecting a subtle difference. Many basic language courses deliberately omit mood particles for the sake of simplicity and it is possible to avoid using them and get by quite adequately. But without mood particles, statements often sound incomplete, abrupt or even impolite. They are best learnt by imitation; everyday conversation, television, dialogue in novels and interviews in newspapers and magazines all provide a ready supply of examples, although the written form of a particle does not always reflect its normal pronunciation. This section discusses some of the most common particles; for a more detailed treatment, see Brown (1969) and Cooke (1989).

10.3.1   dûay (ด้วย)

This particle is typically used in polite requests, apologies and cries for help:

khɔ̌ɔthôot dûay
ขอโทษด้วย
Sorry!

chék bin dûay
เช็คบิลด้วย
Can I have the bill, please?

chûay dûay
ช่วยด้วย
Help!

10.3.2   (ละ)

A contracted form of lɛ́ɛw ('already'), one use of lá is to indicate that a state has been reached (5.7.2):

phɔɔ lá
พอละ
That's enough.

thùuk lá
ถูกละ
That's right/correct.

dii lá
ดีละ
That's fine.

aw lá
เอาละ
OK!; Right, then!

It can also be used to indicate that a situation is about to change (probably representing a contraction of **ca ... léɛw** 'to be about to . . .'):

phǒm klàp bâan lá
ผมกลับบ้านละ
I'm going home.

pay lá
ไปละ
I'm leaving.

ca kin lá
จะกินละ
I'm going to eat.

Another use is with **ìik** ('again') to show mild irritation:

maa ìik lá
มาอีกละ
He's back again.

sǒmchaay ìik lá
สมชายอีกละ
It's Somchai again.

<h2>10.3.3   lâ (ละ́)</h2>

This particle occurs commonly in questions, as a way of pressing for an
answer; in the following two examples, it is common to hear **lâ** reduced
to **â**:

thammay lâ?
ทำไมละ
Why?

pay nǎy lâ?
ไปไหนละ
Where are you going?

Sometimes the particle conveys a sense of irritation, similar to English
'why on earth . . .?':

thammay tɔ̂ŋ pay bɔ̀ɔk kháw lâ?
ทำไมต้องไปบอกเขาละ
Why on earth did you have to go and tell her?

aw pay sɔ̂ɔn wáy thîi nǎy lâ?
เอาไปซ่อนไว้ที่ไหนล่ะ
Where on earth have you gone and hidden it?

It is also used in the pattern lέεw ... lâ ('And how about ...?, What about ...?') to change the focus or topic of conversation:

lέεw khun lâ?
แล้วคุณล่ะ
And how about you?

lέεw phrûŋ níi lâ?
เล้วพรุ่งนี้ล่ะ
And how about tomorrow?

ná (นะ)

This particle often serves to make a sentence milder or less abrupt by seeking approval, agreement or compromise. Commands are similarly made milder and convey a sense of coaxing and urging; ná often corresponds to the use of '..., OK?' or '..., right?' in English:

pay lá ná
ไปละนะ
I'm going now, OK?

chán mây wâa ná
ฉันไม่ว่านะ
I don't mind, OK?

yàa bɔ̀ɔk thəə ná
อย่าบอกเธอนะ
Don't tell her, OK?

ná is also used when requesting someone to repeat a piece of information, similar to English 'What was that again?':

aray ná?
อะไรนะ
Pardon? What was that again?

khray ná?
ใครนะ
Who was that again?

khun klàp mûarày ná?
คุณกลับมาเมื่อไรนะ
When was that again, that you're going back?

Note also the use of **ná** as a question particle when seeking agreement (see 12.1.4).

10.3.5	**nâ/nâa** (น่ะ/น่า)

This particle is used when persuading somebody to do something or accept an idea when they are reluctant (cf. Come on, . . .):

yàa pay nâa
อย่าไปน่า
Oh, come on, don't go.

It is also used to highlight the topic of a sentence, in much the same way that some speakers of English use 'right':

phûuyǐŋ nâ kɔ̂ pen yàaŋ nán
ผู้หญิงน่ะก็เป็นอย่างนั้น
Women, right, are like that.

tɔɔn khruu sɔ̌ɔn yùu nâ phǒm faŋ mây rúu rûaŋ ləəy
ตอนครูสอนอยู่นะผมฟังไม่รู้เรื่องเลย
When the teacher is teaching, right, I don't understand a word.

10.3.6	**nɔ̀y** (หน่อย)

Polite request particle, basically meaning 'just a little'; used to minimise the degree of imposition on the listener; similar in function to **thii** but used much more widely; commonly occurs in requests that begin with **khɔ̌ɔ** or **chûay**:

phûut cháa cháa nɔ̀y dâay máy?
พูดช้าๆ หน่อยได้ไหม
Could you speak slowly, please?

khɔ̌ɔ duu nɔ̀y
ขอดูหน่อย
Could I have a look, please?

chûay pìt thii wii nɔ̀y
ช่วยปิดทีวีหน่อย
Please turn the TV off.

10.3.7 ŋay (ไง)

Often used as a response to a statement or question to show that the respondent thinks the answer is self-evident:

kháw mây yɔɔm khâa man
เขาไม่ยอมฆ่ามัน
He wouldn't kill it.
– kɔ̂ pen bàap ŋay lâ
– ก็เป็นบาปไงล่ะ
– Well, it's sinful, of course.

sɨ̂a chán hǎay pay nǎy?
เสื้อฉันหายไปไหน
Where's my blouse disappeared to?
– nîi ŋay yùu troŋ níi eeŋ
– นี่ไง อยู่ตรงนี้เอง
– Here it is. Right here.

It is also used in the Thai equivalent of 'here you are', used when giving something to someone:

nîi ŋay lâ khráp/khâ
นี่ไงล่ะครับ/ค่ะ
Here you are!

10.3.8 rɔ̀k/lɔ̀k (หรอก)

Occurs most commonly at the end of negative statements to contradict the addressee's statement or belief:

mây tɔ̂ŋ lɔ̀k
ไม่ต้องหรอก
There's no need. (when declining an offer)

phɛɛŋ khráp
แพงครับ
It's expensive.
– mây phɛɛŋ lɔ̀k khâ
– ไม่แพงหรอกค่ะ
– No it isn't.

In positive statements it can convey a qualified or somewhat hesitant acceptance of the addressee's statement or belief:

kɔ̂ ciŋ lɔ̀k
ก็จริงหรอก
That's true (but . . .)

kháw phûut thay kèŋ
เขาพูดไทยเก่ง
He speaks Thai well.

– **kɔ̂ kèŋ lɔ̀k tɛ̀ɛ yaŋ khĭan mây pen**
– ก็เก่งหรอก แต่ยังเขียนไม่เป็น
– Yes . . . but he can't write yet.

It can also be used to express sarcasm:

pen phɔ̂ɔ tua yàaŋ lɔ̀k
เป็นพ่อตัวอย่างหรอก
He's a model parent!

or mild annoyance:

phŏm phûut dâay eeŋ lɔ̀k
ผมพูดได้เองหรอก
I can speak for myself.

10.3.9   sí/sì/sii/sîi (ซิ/สิ/ซี/ซี่)

This particle is most commonly used in commands. When pronounced with a short vowel and followed by a polite particle it does not convey any sense of abruptness and is widely used in polite requests ('Do sit down, please'); more insistent requests and commands are conveyed when the particle is pronounced with a falling tone and longer vowel ('Sit down!'):

chəən nâŋ sí khá
เชิญนั่งซิคะ
Please sit down.

duu sí khráp
ดูซิครับ
Look!, Take a look!

phûut ìik thii sí khá
พูดอีกทีซิคะ
Please say that again.

nâŋ sîi
นั่งซี่
Sit down! (and listen)

pìt pratuu sîi
ปิดประตูซี่
Shut the door! (I've told you once already)

Another use of this particle is to emphasise a positive response to a question:

pay máy?
ไปไหม
Shall we go?
– **pay sii**
– ไปซี
– Yes, let's.

yàak lɔɔŋ máy?
อยากลองไหม
Do you want to try it?
– **yàak sii**
– อยากซี
– Yes, I would.

It is also used to contradict negative statements:

kháw kHoŋ mây maa
เขาคงไม่มา
He probably won't come.
– **maa sii**
– มาซี
– Oh yes, he will!

chán phûut aŋkrìt mây kèŋ
ฉันพูดอังกฤษไม่เก่ง
I don't speak English well.
– **kèŋ sii**
– เก่งซี
– Oh yes, you do!

| 10.3.10 | **thə̀/hə̀** (เถิด/เถอะ/เหอะ) |

A mild, 'urging' particle, used in suggestions, invitations, requests and mild commands; can often be conveyed in English by 'you'd/we'd better

...' , 'why don't you/we ...', 'go ahead and ...', 'let's ...', depending on the context; when it is used to urge someone to do something, a reason is often given, too; when joint activity is being suggested, it is often preceded by **kan** ('together'); often reduced to **hə̀** in informal speech.

klàp bâan thə̀ dὺk lέεw
กลับบ้านเถอะ ดึกแล้ว
You'd better go home. It's late.

pay kin kan thə̀
ไปกินกันเถอะ
Let's go and eat.

dǐaw hə̀
เดี๋ยวเถอะ
Steady on!/Not so fast!

10.3.11 thii (ที)

Polite request particle, basically meaning 'just this once'; used to minimise degree of imposition on listener; similar in function to **nɔ̀y** but much more restricted in use; note the idiomatic **khɔ̌ɔ thii**:

khɔ̌ɔthôot thii
ขอโทษที
Sorry!

khɔ̌ɔ phûut thii
ขอพูดที
Can I say something/get a word in?

chûay pìt thii wii thii
ช่วยปิดทีวีที
Please turn the TV off.

khɔ̌ɔ thii
ขอที
Don't!

Chapter 11

Negation

Negative words in Thai are (a) **mây** ('not, no'), widely used in negative sentences and negative responses to questions; (b) **mí**, a variant of **mây**; (c) **yàa** ('don't') and (d) **hâam** ('to forbid'), both used in negative commands and prohibitions; (e) **plàaw** ('no'), a negative response which contradicts the assumption in the question; and (f) **yaŋ** ('not yet'), used only as a negative response to **. . . rú yaŋ?** questions (12.1.6).

11.1 Negating main verbs

Verbs are generally negated by the pattern **mây + VERB (PHRASE)**:

chán mây pay
ฉันไม่ไป
I'm not going.

aahǎan mây aròy
อาหารไม่อร่อย
The food isn't tasty.

Verb compounds (5.3) also follow this pattern:

chán mây plìan plɛɛŋ
ฉันไม่เปลี่ยนแปลง
I'm not changing.

chán mây duu lɛɛ kháw
ฉันไม่ดูแลเขา
I don't look after her.

For negation of 'to be', see 5.1.

11.2 Negating resultative verbs

Combinations of verb + resultative verbs (5.4) are superficially similar to verb compounds, but are negated by the pattern VERB + (OBJECT) + mây + RESULTATIVE VERB:

raw nɔɔn mây làp
เรานอนไม่หลับ
We didn't sleep.

kháw hǎa mây cəə
เขาหาไม่เจอ
He can't find it.

chán khít mây ɔ̀ɔk
ฉันคิดไม่ออก
I can't work it out.

kháw àan mây khâw cay/mây rúu rɨ̂aŋ
เขาอ่านไม่เข้าใจ/ไม่รู้เรื่อง
He doesn't understand. (what he is reading)

phǒm faŋ mây than
ผมฟังไม่ทัน
I can't keep up. (they're speaking too fast)

bɔ̀ɔk mây thùuk
บอกไม่ถูก
It's hard to say.

chán duu nǎŋ mây còp
ฉันดูหนังไม่จบ
I didn't see the film through to the end.

lûuk kin khâaw mây mòt
ลูกกินข้าวไม่หมด
My kids don't eat up all their rice.

The word **yaŋ** can be added, either immediately before **mây**, or immediately before the main verb, to convey the sense that the action has not yet produced the intended result:

chán duu nǎŋ yaŋ mây còp/chán yaŋ duu nǎŋ mây còp
ฉันดูหนังยังไม่จบ/ฉันยังดูหนังไม่จบ
I haven't yet finished watching the film.

kháw tham ŋaan yaŋ mây sèt/kháw yaŋ tham ŋaan mây sèt

เขาทำงานยังไม่เสร็จ/เขายังทำงานไม่เสร็จ

He hasn't yet finished work.

11.3 Negating auxiliary verbs

There are three patterns for negating auxiliary verbs; note that tɔ̂ŋ (must) can occur in both patterns, but with different meanings:

11.3.1 mây + AUXILIARY VERB + VERB (PHRASE)

A relatively small number of verbs follow this pattern, the most common being:

khəəy	เคย	used to do/be, have ever done/been
khuan (ca)	ควร(จะ)	should/ought
nâa (ca)	น่า(จะ)	should/ought
yàak (ca)	อยาก(จะ)	want to, would like to
tɔ̂ŋ	ต้อง	have to, must

chán mây khəəy kin
ฉันไม่เคยกิน
I've never eaten it.

khun mây khuan (ca) súu
คุณไม่ควร(จะ)ซื้อ
You shouldn't have bought it.

raw mây yàak (ca) klàp bâan
เราไม่อยาก(จะ)กลับบ้าน
We don't want to go home.

khun mây tɔ̂ŋ bɔ̀ɔk kháw
คุณไม่ต้องบอกเขา
You don't have to tell him/There's no need to tell him.

11.3.2 AUXILIARY VERB + mây + VERB (PHRASE)

Auxiliary verbs which follow this pattern include:

ca	จะ	future time marker
àat (ca)	อาจ(จะ)	may/might

khoŋ (ca)	คง(จะ)	will probably, sure to
mák (ca)	มัก(จะ)	tend to, usually
yɔ̂m (ca)	ย่อม(จะ)	likely to
hěn ca	เห็นจะ	seems that
thɛ̂ɛp (ca)	แทบ(จะ)	almost, nearly
thâa ca	ถ้าจะ	might, it could be
thâa thaaŋ (ca)	ท่าทาง(จะ)	look like/as though
duu mǔan (ca)	ดูเหมือน(จะ)	look like/as though
yɔ̂m (ca)	ย่อม(จะ)	likely to, apt to
tɔ̂ŋ	ต้อง	have to, must

phǒm àat ca mây pay
ผมอาจจะไม่ไป
I might not go.

khun khoŋ ca mây sǒn cay
คุณคงจะไม่สนใจ
You probably won't be interested.

kháw mák ca mây chɔ̂ɔp
เขามักจะไม่ชอบ
She usually doesn't like it.

khun tɔ̂ŋ mây bɔ̀ɔk kháw
คุณต้องไม่บอกเขา
You must not tell him.

11.3.3   VERB (PHRASE) + **mây** + AUXILIARY VERB

This pattern occurs with the modal verbs expressing ability and permission, **pen, dâay** and **wǎy** (5.6.2):

kháw phûut thay mây pen
เขาพูดไทยไม่เป็น
He can't speak Thai.

khun pay mây dâay
คุณไปไม่ได้
You can't go.

chán thon mây wăy
ฉันทนไม่ไหว
I can't stand it.

11.4 *mây dây* + VERB (PHRASE)

The pattern, **mây dây** + VERB (PHRASE) is used in the following cases.

11.4.1 To form a negative past with verbs of motion, action, utterance, etc.

It is not used with stative verbs or pre-verbs (5.7.7):

raw mây dây súu
เราไม่ได้ซื้อ
We didn't buy it.

phûan mây dây maa
เพื่อนไม่ได้มา
My friend didn't come.

11.4.2 To contradict an assumption

It does not indicate any particular tense and may refer to past or present:

bâan yùu kruŋthêep lǎǝ?
บ้านอยู่กรุงเทพฯหรือ
Your house is in Bangkok, then?
– **plàaw mây dây yùu kruŋthêep**
– เปล่า ไม่ได้อยู่กรุงเทพฯ
– No, it's not in Bangkok.

kháw pen fɛɛn lǎǝ?
เขาเป็นแฟนหรือ
She's your girlfriend, then?
– **plàaw mây dây pen**
– เปล่า ไม่ได้เป็น
– No, she's not.

khun sɔ̌ɔn phaasǎa aŋkrìt lǒ̌ǝ?
คุณสอนภาษาอังกฤษหรือ
You taught English, then?
– plàaw mây dây sɔ̌ɔn
– เปล่า ไม่ได้สอน
– No, I didn't.

11.4.3   To negate the verbs **chǔǔ** ('to be named') and **pen** ('to be').
See 5.1:

kháw mây dây chǔǔ tɔ̂y
เขาไม่ได้ชื่อต้อย
Her name isn't Toi.

phǒm mây dây pen khon ameerikan
ผมไม่ได้เป็นคนอเมริกัน
I'm not an American.

11.5   *mây chây +* NOUN

mây chây + NOUN negates phrases consisting of the verb **pen** ('to
be') + NOUN (5.1); it is often interchangeable with **mây dây pen** + NOUN.

nîi mây chây bâan kháw
นี่ไม่ใช่บ้านเขา
This isn't his house.

chán pen khruu mây chây mɔ̌ɔ
ฉันเป็นครูไม่ใช่หมอ
I'm a teacher, not a doctor.

kháw mây chây phǔan
เขาไม่ใช่เพื่อน
He's not a friend.

'It is neither . . ., nor . . .', is expressed by the pattern NOUN 1 + kɔ̂ mây
chây + NOUN 2 + kɔ̂ mây chǝǝŋ:

phàk kɔ̂ mây chây phǒnlamáay kɔ̂ mây chǝǝŋ
ผักก็ไม่ใช่ ผลไม้ก็ไม่เชิง
It's neither vegetable, nor fruit.

11.6   mây mii

mây mii ('there are not') is placed before a noun to form the negative
quantifier 'not any' and 'no':

mây mii rót mee
ไม่มีรถเมล์
There aren't any buses.

mây mii phûan maa yîam chán
ไม่มีเพื่อนมาเยี่ยมฉัน
No friends came to visit me.

mây mii is also used to negate the indefinite pronouns **khray** ('anyone')
aray ('anything') and **thîi nǎy** ('anywhere'):

mây mii khray rúu
ไม่มีใครรู้
No one knows.

mây mii aray kə̀ət khûn
ไม่มีอะไรเกิดขึ้น
Nothing happened.

mây mii thîi nǎy thîi mɔ̀
ไม่มีที่ไหนที่เหมาะ
There's nowhere suitable.

11.7   Modifying negatives: intensifying and softening

Negative statements are intensified or softened by using a 'wrap-around'
construction in which the verb occurs between the negative word and the
modifier: **mây** + VERB (PHRASE) + INTENSIFIER/SOFTENER.

Common negative intensifiers are:

mây . . . ləəy	ไม่ . . . เลย	not at all . . .
mây . . . nɛ̂ɛ	ไม่ . . . แน่	not . . . for sure
mây . . . dèt khàat	ไม่ . . . เด็ดขาด	absolutely not . . .

chán mây chɔ̂ɔp ləəy
ฉันไม่ชอบเลย
I don't like it at all.

kháw mây maa nêɛ
เขาไม่มาแน่
He is not coming for sure.

A more elaborate pattern is **mây . . . mɛ́ɛ tɛ̀ɛ** + CLASSIFIER + **diaw** ('not
. . ., not even a single . . .'):

phǒm mây rúucàk khray mɛ́ɛ tɛ̀ɛ khon diaw
ผมไม่รู้จักใครแม้แต่คนเดียว
I don't know even a single person.

kháw mây sǒn cay mɛ́ɛ tɛ̀ɛ nít diaw
เขาไม่สนใจแม้แต่นิดเดียว
He is not even the slightest bit interested.

Common softeners are:

mây (khɔ̌y) . . . thâwrày	ไม่(ค่อย) . . . เท่าไร	not very . . .
mây (khɔ̌y) . . . nák	ไม่(ค่อย) . . . นัก	not very . . .
mây (sûu) . . . nák	ไม่(สู้) . . . นัก	not very . . .

nǎŋ mây khɔ̌y sanùk thâwrày
หนังไม่ค่อยสนุกเท่าไร
The film wasn't much fun.

mây khɔ̌y also commonly occurs without **thâwrày** or **nák**:

chán mây khɔ̌y chɔ̂ɔp
ฉันไม่ค่อยชอบ
I don't like it very much.

11.8 Negative imperatives

Negative commands follow the pattern, **yàa** ('Don't') + VERB (PHRASE),
or **hâam** ('It's forbidden to . . .') + VERB (PHRASE); both can be made
more emphatic ('absolutely not, under no circumstances, don't ever . . .')
by adding **pen an khàat** or **dèt khàat** after the verb or verb phrase, or
modified in various other ways by the addition of mood particles (10.3).
See also 15.4.5.

yàa/hâam bɔ̀ɔk kháw (ná)
อย่า/ห้ามบอกเขา(นะ)
Don't tell him (right?).

145

yàa/hâam thoo maa ìik pen an khàat
อย่า/ห้ามโทรมาอีกเป็นอันขาด
Don't ever, under any circumstances, ring me again.

The pattern, **yàa phôŋ** + VERB (PHRASE) conveys the sense that it is the wrong time for doing something:

yàa phôŋ pìt ɛɛ ná
อย่าเพิ่งปิดแอร์นะ
Don't turn the air-conditioning off just yet, OK?

yàa phôŋ bɔ̀ɔk kháw ná
อย่าเพิ่งบอกเขานะ
Don't tell him just yet, OK?

yàa phôŋ
อย่าเพิ่ง
Not now!

11.9   Negative causatives

Causative constructions (5.11) are negated according to the following patterns.

11.9.1   SUBJECT (human/non-human) + **mây** + **tham** + (inanimate OBJECT) + VERB

khɔ̌ɔ yʉʉm nɔ̀y ca mây tham sǐa
ขอยืมหน่อย จะไม่ทำเสีย
Can I borrow it? I won't damage it.

phǒm mây dây tham tɛ̀ɛk khráp
ผมไม่ได้ทำแตกครับ
I didn't break it.

Note that **mây dây** is used instead of **mây** to negate actions in the past (5.7.7).

11.9.2   SUBJECT (human) + **mây** + **hây** + (animate OBJECT) + VERB (PHRASE)

kháw mây hây phanrayaa tham ŋaan
เขาไม่ให้ภรรยาทำงาน
He doesn't let his wife work.

phɔ̂ɔ mây hây lûuk klàp bâan dɯ̀k

พ่อไม่ให้ลูกกลับบ้านดึก

The father doesn't let his children come home late.

raw mây dây hây kháw maa

เราไม่ได้ให้เขามา

We didn't let him come.

When **hây** is preceded by a specifying verb, such as **bɔ̀ɔk** ('to tell'), the negative can take two distinct forms and meanings, depending on whether it is the specifying verb or **hây** which is being negated.

11.9.3 SUBJECT (human) + specifying verb + **mây** + **hây** + (animate OBJECT) + VERB (PHRASE)

kháw bɔ̀ɔk mây hây chán cháy ŋən mâak

เขาบอกไม่ให้ฉันใช้เงินมาก

He told me not to spend a lot of money.

mia tɯan mây hây kháw klàp bâan dɯ̀k

เมียเตือนไม่ให้เขากลับบ้านดึก

His wife warned him not to come home late.

phɔ̂ɔ hâam mây hây chán kin lâw

พ่อห้ามไม่ให้ฉันกินเหล้า

My father forbids me to drink alcohol.

hǔa nâa pàtìsèet mây hây phǒm laa pùay

หัวหน้าปฏิเสธไม่ให้ผมลาป่วย

My boss refuses to let me take sick leave.

Alternatively, the object can occur after the specifying verb and before **mây hây**:

kháw bɔ̀ɔk chán mây hây cháy ŋən mâak

เขาบอกไม่ให้ฉันใช้เงินมาก

He told me not to spend a lot of money.

phɔ̂ɔ hâam chán mây hây kin lâw

พ่อห้ามฉันไม่ให้กินเหล้า

My father forbids me to drink alcohol.

Note that in negative causative constructions **pàtìsèet** ('to refuse') and **hâam** ('forbid') occur with **mây hây** (and not **hây** on its own), creating an apparent 'double negative' ('refuse not to let', 'forbid not to let'). It should also be noted that **hâam** can occur without **hây**, both in simple causative sentences and in negative imperatives (11.8):

phôɔ hâam chán kin lâw
พอห้ามฉันกินเหล้า
My father forbids me to drink alcohol.

hâam pɔ̀ɔt pratuu
ห้ามเปิดประตู
Don't open the door!

| 11.9.4 | SUBJECT (human) + **mây** + specifying verb + **hây** + (animate OBJECT) + VERB (PHRASE) |

mɛ̂ɛ mây anúyâat hây lûuk pay rooŋ rian
แม่ไม่อนุญาตให้ลูกไปโรงเรียน
The mother does not allow her children to go to school.

chán mây yɔɔm hây kháw tham yàaŋ nán
ฉันไม่ยอมให้เขาทำอย่างนั้น
I don't let him do that.

kháw mây dây tɨan hây raw rawaŋ khamooy
เขาไม่ได้เตือนให้เราระวังขโมย
He didn't warn us to watch out for burglars.

| 11.9.5 | SUBJECT (human or non-human) + **mây** + **tham hây** + (OBJECT) + VERB (PHRASE) |

rót tìt yuŋ kàt mây tham hây chán dɨat rɔ́ɔn
รถติดยุงกัดไม่ทำให้ฉันเดือดร้อน
Traffic jams and mosquito bites don't bother me.

tɨ̀ɨn sǎay mây tham hây pay tham ŋaan cháa
ตื่นสายไม่ทำให้ไปทำงานช้า
Getting up late doesn't make me late for work.

11.10 Negative questions

Negative questions ('You didn't . . . did you?') are formed according to the following patterns:

(a)   **mây** + VERB + **lɵ̌ɵ?**

(b)   **mây** + VERB + **chây máy?**

(c)   SUBJECT + VERB + **mây chây lɵ̌ɵ?**

Note that the question word **máy?** (12.1.1) is not used in negative questions.

Negative questions present a problem for English speakers in that yes/no answers are reversed in Thai: where in English, we say 'No (I didn't)' and 'Yes (I did)', Thai has 'Yes (I didn't)' and 'No (I did)'. In replying to negative questions, providing additional clarification to a yes/no response (shown in brackets in the examples) can pre-empt misunderstandings:

khun mây sʉ́ʉ lɔ̌ɔ?
คุณไม่ซื้อหรือ
You're not buying it, right?
– **khráp (mây sʉ́ʉ)/sʉ́ʉ sii khâ**
– ครับ (ไม่ซื้อ)/ซื้อสิค่ะ
– No (I'm not)/Yes, I am.

khun mây rúu chây máy?
คุณไม่รู้ใช่ไหม
You don't know, right?
– **chây (mây rúu)/mây chây (rúu)**
– ใช่ (ไม่รู้)/ไม่ใช่ (รู้)
– No (I don't)/Yes (I do).

nîi rót khɔ̌ɔŋ khun mây chây lɔ̌ɔ?
นี่รถของคุณไม่ใช่หรือ
This is your car, isn't it?
– **chây (khɔ̌ɔŋ phǒm)/mây chây**
– ใช่ (ของผม)/ไม่ใช่
– Yes (it's mine)/No.

For negative why? questions ('why didn't you ..?') see 12.2.7.

11.11 Negative conditional clauses

Negative conditional clauses ('unless, otherwise if . . . not') are introduced by **mây yàaŋ nán** ('otherwise'), often shortened to **mây yaŋ nán** or **mây ŋán**, **míchànán** ('otherwise') or simply **mây**; as in positive conditional clauses (9.2.1), the word **thâa** ('if') is frequently omitted:

mây yàaŋ nán raw ca pay ráp
ไม่อย่างนั้นเราจะไปรับ
Otherwise we'll go and pick (her) up.

míchànán phǒm mây pay
มิฉะนั้นผมไม่ไป
Otherwise I'm not going.

mây yàak pay kɔ̂ mây tɔ̂ŋ

ไม่อยากไปก็ไม่ต้อง

If you don't want to go, (you) don't have to.

mây bɔ̀ɔk kɔ̂ chûay mây dâay

ไม่บอกก็ช่วยไม่ได้

Unless (you) tell (me), (I) can't help.

mây chây wan níi kɔ̂ tɔ̂ŋ pen phrûŋ níi

ไม่ใช่วันนี้ก็ต้องเป็นพรุ่งนี้

If not today, then it must be tomorrow.

11.12 Saying 'no'

The negative answer to a yes/no question is determined by the question particle. Thus, for example, a 'no' answer to a question that ends in . . . máy? is mây + VERB (PHRASE) , while for a question ending in . . . lɛ́ɛw rɯ́ yaŋ?, it is yaŋ. Yes/no answers are dealt with in more detail in 12.1, but the following table provides a basic summary of the most likely negative responses:

Questions ending in:	NO answer
. . . máy?	mây + VERB
. . . lɔ̌ɔ?	mây (+ POLITE PARTICLE)
	mây + VERB
	plàaw
. . . chây máy?	mây chây
	mây chəəŋ
. . . lɛ́ɛw rɯ́ yaŋ?	yaŋ (+ POLITE PARTICLE)
	yaŋ mây + VERB
. . . rɯ́ plàaw?	mây + VERB
	plàaw
. . . ná?	mây + VERB

Note also the more qualified 'no' response, **mây chəəŋ** ('not really, not exactly, I wouldn't say that'):

nâa bə̀a mâak máy?
น่าเบื่อมากไหม
Was it very boring?
– **kɔ̂ mây chəəŋ**
– ก็ไม่เชิง
– Well, not exactly.

11.13 Useful negative expressions

mây pen ray	ไม่เป็นไร	never mind!
mây mii thaaŋ	ไม่มีทาง	no way!
mây mii wan	ไม่มีวัน	never!
mây mii panhǎa	ไม่มีปัญหา	no problem!; without question
cháy mây dâay	ใช้ไม่ได้	(it's) no good
mây pen rə̂aŋ	ไม่เป็นเรื่อง	(it's) nonsense
mây khâw rə̂aŋ	ไม่เข้าเรื่อง	(it's) irrelevant
mây aw nǎy	ไม่เอาไหน	(it's) useless, good-for-nothing
pen pay mây dâay	เป็นไปไม่ได้	(it's) impossible
mây kìaw	ไม่เกี่ยว	(it's) irrelevant

kháw phûut mây pen rə̂aŋ
เขาพูดไม่เป็นเรื่อง
He's talking nonsense.

kháw pen khon mây aw nǎy
เขาเป็นคนไม่เอาไหน
He's a good-for-nothing.

11.14 Two further negatives: *mí* and *hǎa . . . mây*

Two other negative forms to be aware of, which are most likely to be encountered in written Thai, are **mí**, a polite, rather formal variant of

151

mây, and the 'wrap-around' expression, hǎa + VERB (PHRASE) + mây, which can seriously mislead the unsuspecting learner:

kháw tham dooy mí dây wǎŋ prayòot aray
เขาทำโดยมิได้หวังประโยชน์อะไร
He did it without hoping for any benefit.

kháw hǎa dây còp mahǎawítthayaalay mây
เขาหาได้จบมหาวิทยาลัยไม่
He did not graduate from university.

Chapter 12

Questions

12.1 Yes/no questions

Statements are transformed into questions that require a simple yes/no answer by adding the question particles, **máy?**, **lɔ̌ə?**, **chây máy?**, **ná?**, **rɯ́ plàaw?** or **rɯ́ yaŋ?**, to the end of the statement:

statement	*question*
aahǎan yîipùn phɛɛŋ	**aahǎan yîipùn phɛɛŋ máy?**
อาหารญี่ปุ่นแพง	อาหารญี่ปุ่นแพงไหม
Japanese food is expensive.	Is Japanese food expensive?
kháw pen phɯ̂an	**kháw pen phɯ̂an chây máy?**
เขาเป็นเพื่อน	เขาเป็นเพื่อนใช่ไหม
He's a friend.	He's a friend, is he?

There is no single word for 'yes' and for 'no'; the appropriate way of saying yes/no is determined by the question particle used.

12.1.1 ... máy? questions

máy? is an information-seeking question particle used in neutral questions which do not anticipate either a positive or negative response. Answers to simple **máy?** questions are formed as follows:

Yes: VERB

No: **mây** + VERB

klay máy?
ไกลไหม
Is it far?

– **klay/mây klay**
– ไกล/ไม่ไกล
– Yes/No.

If the question includes more than one verb, the first verb is normally used in responses:

yàak pay duu năŋ máy?
อยากไปดูหนังไหม
Would you like to go and see a film?
– **yàak/mây yàak**
– อยาก/ไม่อยาก
– Yes/No.

Although the question particle **máy?** is written in Thai script as if it had a rising tone, in normal speech it is pronounced with a high tone. Note that **máy?** when used alone does not occur in negative questions (11.10).

| 12.1.2 | **... lə̆ə/rʉ̌ʉ? questions**

lə̆ə? is a confirmation-seeking question particle used in questions which make an assumption and seek confirmation of that assumption. Answers to **lə̆ə?** questions are formed as follows:

Yes: **khráp/khâ** (+ VERB)
      or
      VERB + **khráp/khâ**

No: **mây** + VERB
      or
      plàaw + khráp/khâ (+ **mây** + VERB) *

*Note **plàaw** conveys a stronger sense of denying the assumption made in the question; to avoid abruptness, it may be followed by a further clarifying statement.

kháw chɔ̂ɔp lə̆ə?
เขาชอบหรือ
He likes it, does he?
– **khráp chɔ̂ɔp**
– ครับ ชอบ
– Yes.
– **mây chɔ̂ɔp/plàaw khâ mây chɔ̂ɔp ləəy**
–ไม่ชอบ/เปล่าค่ะ ไม่ชอบเลย
– No./No, he doesn't like it at all.

lɔ̌ə? commonly occurs in negative questions (11.10) and in isolation, where it means 'Really?'; it is written in Thai script as if it were pronounced **rɯ̌ɯ**, although this pronunciation is seldom heard.

12.1.3 . . . chây máy? *questions*

chây máy? questions are similar to lɔ̌ə? questions (12.1.2) in that they seek confirmation of the assumption made in the question. Answers to chây máy? questions are formed as follows:

Yes: **chây**

No: **mây chây**

mɛ̂ɛ pen khon thay chây máy?
แม่เป็นคนไทยใช่ไหม
Your mother is Thai, isn't she?
– **chây/mây chây**
– ใช่/ไม่ใช่
– Yes/No.

châi máy? also commonly occurs in negative questions (11.10).

12.1.4 . . . ná? *questions*

ná? is an agreement-seeking question particle used in questions which invite agreement with the preceding statement (e.g. It's a nice day today, isn't it?), rather than to confirm whether or not the statement is true; it is commonly used in conversation-initiating questions. (For other uses of ná, see 10.3.) Answers to ná? questions are formed as follows:

Yes: **khráp/khâ**
or
VERB + **khráp/khâ**

No: **mây** + VERB + **khráp/khâ**

wan níi rɔ́ɔn ná?
วันนี้ร้อนนะ
It's hot today, isn't it?
– **khâ (khráp)/rɔ́ɔn khâ (khráp)**
– ค่ะ(ครับ)/ร้อนค่ะ(ครับ)
– Yes.
mây rɔ́ɔn khâ (khráp)
ไม่ร้อนค่ะ(ครับ)
– No.

12.1.5 ... rɯ́ plàaw? *questions*

rɯ́ plàaw? questions, although not as brusque as the English translation ('. . . or not?') suggests, demand a straight 'yes' or 'no' answer. Answers to rɯ́ plàaw? questions are formed as follows:

If the question refers to the present or future:

Yes: VERB

No: **mây** + VERB
       or
       plàaw (+ **mây** + VERB)

khun ca pay rɯ́ plàaw?
คุณจะไปหรือเปล่า
Are you going (or not)?
– **pay/mây pay**
– ไป/ไม่ไป
– Yes/No.

kháw bɯ̀a rɯ́ plàaw?
เขาเบื่อหรือเปล่า
Is he bored (or not)?
– **bɯ̀a/mây bɯ̀a** or **plàaw mây bɯ̀a**
– เบื่อ/ไม่เบื่อ or เปล่า ไม่เบื่อ
– Yes/No.

If the question refers to the past, stative verbs (5.2) behave differently to other verbs:

Yes: VERB + **lέεw**
       or
       STATIVE VERB (+ **khráp/khâ**)

No: **mây dây** + VERB
       or
       plàaw + **khráp/khâ** (+ **mây dây** + VERB)
       or
       mây + STATIVE VERB
       or
       plàaw + **khráp/khâ** (+ **mây** + STATIVE VERB)

khun bɔ̀ɔk kháw rɨ́ plàaw?
คุณบอกเขาหรือเปล่า
Did you tell him (or not)?
– **bɔ̀ɔk lɛ́ɛw/mây dây bɔ̀ɔk**
– บอกแล้ว/ไม่ได้บอก
– Yes/No.

khun bɨ̀a rɨ́ plàaw?
คุณเบื่อหรือเปล่า
Were you bored (or not)?
– **bɨ̀a/mây bɨ̀a** or **plàaw khráp (khâ) mây bɨ̀a.**
– เบื่อ/ไม่เบื่อ or เปล่าครับ(ค่ะ) ไม่เบื่อ
– Yes/No.

As an alternative to **rɨ́ plàaw?** ('. . . or not?') questions can also be formed using **rɨ́ mây?**; answers follow the same pattern as for **rɨ́ plàaw?** questions:

khun ca pay rɨ́ mây?
คุณจะไปหรือไม่
Are you going or not?

Note that **rɨ́** in **rɨ́ plàaw?** and **rɨ́ yaŋ?** (12.1.6) is spelt as if it were pronounced **rɨ̌ɨ**.

12.1.6 . . . (lɛ́ɛw) rɨ́ yaŋ? *questions*

(**lɛ́ɛw**) **rɨ́ yaŋ?** questions ask whether something has happened yet; the word **lɛ́ɛw** ('already') is often omitted in spoken Thai. Answers to (**lɛ́ɛw**) **rɨ́ yaŋ?** questions are formed as follows, with the negative response **yaŋ** often expanded to avoid sounding too abrupt:

Yes: VERB + **lɛ́ɛw**

No: **yaŋ khráp/khâ** expanded by
      either
      yaŋ mây dây + VERB
      or
      yaŋ mây + STATIVE VERB

kin khâaw (lɛ́ɛw) rɨ́ yaŋ?
กินข้าว(แล้ว)หรือยัง
Have you eaten yet?
– **kin lɛ́ɛw/yaŋ khráp(khâ) yaŋ mây dây kin**
– กินแล้ว/ยังครับ(ค่ะ) ยังไม่ได้กิน
– Yes/No, I haven't.

phɔɔ (lɛ́ɛw) rɚ́ yaŋ?

พอ(แล้ว)หรือยัง

Is that enough?

– **phɔɔ lɛ́ɛw/yaŋ yaŋ mây phɔɔ**

– พอแล้ว/ยัง ยังไม่พอ

– Yes/No.

(lɛ́ɛw) rɚ́ yaŋ? questions are also used to ask whether someone is married or has children:

khun tɛ̀ŋ ŋaan (lɛ́ɛw) rɚ́ yaŋ?

คุณแต่งงาน(แล้ว)หรือยัง

Are you married?

– **tɛ̀ŋ lɛ́ɛw/yaŋ khráp yaŋ mây tɛ̀ŋ**

– แต่งแล้ว/ยังครับ ยังไม่แต่ง

– Yes/No, I'm not.

kháw mii lûuk (lɛ́ɛw) rɚ́ yaŋ?

เขามีลูก(แล้ว)หรือยัง

Do they have any children?

– **mii lɛ́ɛw/yaŋ khráp yaŋ mây mii**

– มีแล้ว/ยังครับ ยังไม่มี

– Yes/No, they don't.

Note that **rɚ́** is spelt as if it were pronounced **rɯ̌ɯ**.

12.1.7 **ca . . . rɚ́ yaŋ?** *questions*

Superficially similar to (lɛ́ɛw) **rɚ́ yaŋ?** questions (see 12.1.6) are those that have the pattern **ca** + VERB + **rɚ́ yaŋ?** This construction refers not to past actions, but conveys the meaning 'Do you want to . . . yet?' or 'Are you ready to . . . yet?' Answers to **ca** + VERB + **rɚ́ yaŋ?** questions are formed as follows:

Yes: VERB

   or

   ca + VERB + **lɛ́ɛw**

No: **yaŋ khráp/khâ**

   or

   yaŋ mây + VERB

ca kin rɨ́ yaŋ?

จะกินหรือยัง

Are you ready to eat yet?

– **kin** or **ca kin lɛ́ɛw/yaŋ khráp yaŋ mây kin**

– กิน or จะกินแล้ว/ยังครับ ยังไม่กิน

– Yes/No, not yet.

ca klàp bâan rɨ́ yaŋ?

จะกลับบ้านหรือยัง

Are you ready to go home yet?

– **klàp** or **ca klàp lɛ́ɛw/yaŋ khâ yaŋ mây klàp**

– กลับ or จะกลับแล้ว/ยังค่ะ ยังไม่กลับ

– Yes/No, not yet.

12.2 Wh- questions

In English the Wh- question words (who?, what?, where?, why?, when?, which?, how?) normally occur at the beginning of the question. In Thai the position of some question words varies according to their grammatical function in the sentence, while others have a fixed position.

Most Wh- questions are answered by substituting the response word in the position in the sentence that the question word occupies.

Many of the Wh- question words also function as indefinite pronouns ('anyone', 'anything', etc., see 4.8).

12.2.1 Who? questions

The position of the question word **khray?** ('who?') is determined by its grammatical function in the sentence; if the question pattern is VERB + **khray?**, then the answer will be (VERB) + PERSON, while if the question is **khray?** + VERB (PHRASE), the answer will be PERSON + (VERB (PHRASE)):

khun pay kàp khray?

คุณไปกับใคร

Who are you going with?

– **(pay) kàp phɨ̂an**

– (ไป)กับเพื่อน

– With a friend.

khray sɔ̌ɔn?
ใครสอน
Who taught you?
- **aacaan maanát (sɔ̌ɔn)**
- Acharn Manat (did).
- อาจารย์มานัส(สอน)

12.2.2 Whose? questions

Whose? questions are formed by the pattern NOUN + (khɔ̌ɔŋ) + khray
(see also 3.5.12); when there is a preceding noun, **khɔ̌ɔŋ** ('of') is often
omitted; if there is no preceding noun, however, it may not be omitted:

bâan (khɔ̌ɔŋ) khray?
บ้าน(ของ)ใคร
Whose house?
- **bâan (khɔ̌ɔŋ) raw/khɔ̌ɔŋ raw**
- บ้าน(ของ)เรา/ของเรา
- Our house/Ours.

nîi khɔ̌ɔŋ khray?
นี่ของใคร
Whose is this?
- **khɔ̌ɔŋ phǒm**
- ของผม
- It's mine.

12.2.3 What? questions

What? questions are formed using the pattern VERB (PHRASE) + **aray?**
('what?'); note, however, that **aray?** occurs before the aspect marker **yùu**
(5.7.3) and directional verbs (5.5):

kháw chʉ̂ʉ aray?
เขาชื่ออะไร
What's her name?
- **chʉ̂ʉ tɔ̌y**
- ชื่อตอย
- Her name is Toi.

khun tham aray yùu?
คุณทำอะไรอยู่
What are you doing?
– **duu thii wii yùu**
– ดูทีวีอยู่
– Watching TV.

khun súu aray maa?
คุณซื้ออะไรมา
What did you buy?

kòət aray khûn?
เกิดอะไรขึ้น
What's happening?

Note also the common idiomatic expression:

aray kan?
อะไรกัน
What's up?

Some English 'What?' questions use **yaŋŋay?** ('How?') rather than **aray** (see 12.2.8).

12.2.4 Which? questions

Which? questions are formed using the pattern VERB + (NOUN) + CLAS-SIFIER + **nǎy?** ('which?'):

aw náŋsúu lêm nǎy?
เอาหนังสือเล่มไหน
Which book do you want?
– **aw lêm nán**
– เอาเล่มนั้น
– I want that one.

khun khuy kàp phûuyǐŋ khon nǎy?
คุณคุยกับผู้หญิงคนไหน
Which girl did you chat with?
– **(khuy kàp) khon yîipùn**
– (คุยกับ)คนญี่ปุ่น
– (I chatted with) the Japanese one.

kháw klàp wan nǎy?

เขากลับวันไหน

Which day is he returning?

– (klàp) wan aathít

– (กลับ)วันอาทิตย์

– (He is returning) on Sunday.

Where? questions

Where? questions are formed using the pattern VERB (PHRASE) + **thîi nǎy?** ('where?'); **thîi nǎy?** always occurs at the end of a sentence. Answers follow the pattern (VERB (PHRASE) +) **thîi** + LOCATION:

khun phák yùu thîi nǎy?

คุณพักอยู่ที่ไหน

Where are you staying?

– (phák yùu) thîi rooŋ rɛɛm riinoo

– (พักอยู่)ที่โรงแรมรีโน

– (I'm staying) at the Reno Hotel.

kháw kə̀ət thîi nǎy?

เขาเกิดที่ไหน

Where was he born?

– (kə̀ət) thîi kruŋthêep

– (เกิด)ที่กรุงเทพฯ

– (He was born) in Bangkok.

In both questions and answers, **thîi** is normally dropped when the preceding verb is **pay** ('to go') or **maa càak** ('to come from'); in spoken Thai **thîi** is also often dropped when the preceding verb is **yùu** ('to be situated at'):

pay nǎy?

ไปไหน

Where are you going?

– pay sɯ́ɯ khɔ̌ɔŋ

– ไปซื้อของ

– I'm going shopping.

kháw maa càak nǎy?

เขามาจากไหน

Where does he come from?

– **(maa càak) chiaŋmày**

– (มาจาก)เชียงใหม่

– (He comes from) Chiangmai.

bâan yùu nǎy?

บ้านอยู่ไหน

Where is your house?

– **yùu thanǒn sùkhǔmwít**

– อยู่ถนนสุขุมวิท

– It's on Sukhumwit Road.

When? questions

When? questions are formed using the pattern VERB (PHRASE) + mûarày? ('when?'); answers follow the pattern VERB (PHRASE) + EXPRESSION OF TIME. mûarày? normally occurs at the end of a sentence, but may occur at the beginning for emphatic effect:

khun klàp mûarày?

คุณกลับเมื่อไร

When are you returning?

– **(klàp) aathít nâa**

– (กลับ)อาทิตย์หน้า

– (I'm returning) next week.

khun ca bɔ̀ɔk kháw mûarày?

คุณจะบอกเขาเมื่อไร

When are you going to tell her?

mûarày khun ca bɔ̀ɔk kháw?

เมื่อไรคุณจะบอกเขา

When are you going to tell her?

Why? questions

Why? questions are formed using the basic pattern **thammay** ('why?') + (SUBJECT) + (**thǔŋ**) + VERB (PHRASE); the word **thǔŋ**, a colloquial variant of **cuŋ** ('therefore') is optional but extremely common in spoken

Thai. Negative why? questions ('Why doesn't he ...?') follow a similar pattern: **thammay** + (SUBJECT) + (**thǔŋ**) + **mây** ('not') + VERB (PHRASE). Why? questions are answered by **phrɔ́** (**wâa**) ('because') + VERB (PHRASE):

thammay thǔŋ sɯ́ɯ?
ทำไมถึงซื้อ
Why did you buy it?
– **phrɔ́ (wâa) thùuk**
– เพราะ(ว่า)ถูก
– Because it was cheap.

thammay kháw thǔŋ mây kin?
ทำไมเขาถึงไม่กิน
Why didn't he eat it?
– **phrɔ́ (wâa) phèt pay**
– เพราะ(ว่า)เผ็ดไป
– Because it was too spicy.

thammay? can also occur at the end of the sentence, usually in an informal context:

bɔ̀ɔk thammay?
บอกทำไม
Why did you tell her?

To ask 'Why?' in response to a statement, the final particle **lâ?** (see10.3.3) is frequently added:

chán plìan cay lέɛw
ฉันเปลี่ยนใจแล้ว
I've changed my mind.
– **thammay lâ?**
– ทำไมล่ะ
– Why?

12.2.8 | **How? questions: manner**

How? questions in English can be divided into those of manner ('How did you get there?') and those of degree ('How long is it?'); the latter are dealt with in 12.2.9.

Questions of manner follow the pattern VERB (PHRASE) + ya**ŋŋay?** ('how?'); ya**ŋŋay?** is written as if it were spelt yàaŋray, but in informal speech the normal pronunciation ya**ŋŋay?** may be reduced to simply **ŋay?**.

kin yaŋŋay?
กินอย่างไร
How do you eat it?

khĭan yaŋŋay?
เขียนอย่างไร
How do you write it?

pen ŋay?
เป็นอย่างไร
How are things?

ya**ŋŋay?** is sometimes used when English uses 'What?':

khun wâa yaŋŋay?
คุณว่าอย่างไร
What do you think?

khun ca tham yaŋŋay?
คุณจะทำอย่างไร
What will you do?

12.2.9 How? questions: degree

Some questions of degree, such as How tall?, How long (in time)?, How long (in measurement)? and How wide? follow the pattern MEASURE WORD + **thâwrày?** ('how much?'); such questions anticipate a specific numerical response, such as '1.65 metres', '2 hours', etc.

khun pay naan thâwrày?
คุณไปนานเท่าไร
How long are you going for?

nàk thâwrày?
หนักเท่าไร
How heavy is it?

sŭuŋ thâwrày?
สูงเท่าไร
How tall is it?

How? questions which do not necessarily anticipate a precise numerical quantification in the response can be formed by the pattern VERB (PHRASE) + **mâak khɛ̂ɛ nǎy?** ('to what extent?'):

bɨ̀a mâak khɛ̂ɛ nǎy?
เบื่อมากแค่ไหน
How bored were you?

– **bɨ̀a mâak ciŋ ciŋ**
– เบื่อมากจริงๆ
– I was really bored.

sǔay mâak khɛ̂ɛ nǎy?
สวยมากแค่ไหน
How good-looking is she?

– **kɔ̂ɔ . . . sǔay mɨ̆an kan**
– ก็ . . . สวยเหมือนกัน
– Well . . . quite good-looking.

phɛɛŋ mâak khɛ̂ɛ nǎy?
แพงมากแค่ไหน
How expensive is it?

– **phɛɛŋ mâak yàaŋ mây nâa chɨ̀a**
– แพงมากอย่างไม่น่าเชื่อ
– Unbelievably expensive.

12.2.10 How much? questions

How much? questions are formed using the pattern VERB (PHRASE) + **thâwràay?** ('how much?'). **thâwràay?** always occurs at the end of the question:

nîi thâwràay?
นี่เท่าไร
How much is this?

khun sɨ́ɨ thâwràay?
คุณซื้อเท่าไร
How much did you buy it for?

kháw khǎay bâan thâwràay?
เขาขายบ้านเท่าไร
How much did they sell the house for?

Questions which ask 'how much per . . . ?', are formed using the pattern
(NOUN +) CLASSIFIER + la thâwrày? (see also 13.11):

sôm loo la thâwrày?
ส้มโลละเท่าไร
How much are oranges a kilo?

dʉan la thâwrày?
เดือนละเท่าไร
How much a month?

khon la thâwrày?
คนละเท่าไร
How much per person?

How many? questions

How many? questions follow the pattern VERB + (NOUN) + kìi ('how
many?') + CLASSIFIER; the answer normally consists of NUMBER +
CLASSIFIER:

aw kaafɛɛ kìi thûay?
เอากาแฟกี่ถ้วย
How many cups of coffee do you want?
– **sɔ̌ɔŋ thûay**
– สองถ้วย
– Two.

mii lûuk kìi khon?
มีลูกกี่คน
How many children do you have?
– **sǎam khon**
– สามคน
– Three.

pay kìi wan?
ไปกี่วัน
How many days are you going for?
– **cèt wan**
– เจ็ดวัน
– Seven.

12.2.12 *Wh- questions + dii*

The pattern VERB (PHRASE) + WH- QUESTION + **dii** is used for asking advice:

s**ʉʉ aray dii?**
ซื้ออะไรดี
What shall I/we buy?

pay m**ʉaràry dii?**
ไปเมื่อไรดี
When shall I/we go?

tham ya**ŋŋay dii?**
ทำอย่างไรดี
What shall I/we do?

phûut ya**ŋŋay dii?**
พูดอย่างไรดี
How shall I say it?/What shall I say?

12.2.13 *Wh- questions + bâaŋ*

The pattern VERB (PHRASE) + WH- QUESTION + **bâaŋ** anticipates a list of things, people, places, etc. in the response; the list is normally expressed as X + Y + **lɛ́ɛw kɔ̂** ('and') + Z:

kháw s**ʉʉ aray bâaŋ?**
เขาซื้ออะไรบ้าง
What (plural) did he buy?
– **(s****ʉʉ) phàk khǐŋ lɛ́ɛw kɔ̂ plaa**
– (ซื้อ)ผัก ขิง แล้วก็ปลา
– (He bought) vegetables, ginger and fish.

khuy kàp khray bâaŋ?
คุยกับใครบ้าง
Who (plural) did you chat with?
– **(khuy kàp) nók úut lɛ́ɛw kɔ̂ cíap**
– (คุยกับ)นก อู๊ด แล้วก็เจี๊ยบ
– (I chatted with) Nok, Oot and Jiap.

khun pay thîaw thîi nǎy bâaŋ?
คุณไปเที่ยวที่ไหนบ้าง
Where (plural) did you go?

– **(pay thîaw) laaw phamâa lɛ́ɛw kɔ̂ ciin**

– (ไปเที่ยว)ลาว พม่า แล้วก็จีน

– (I went to) Laos, Burma and China.

The question **pen yaŋŋay bâaŋ?** ('How are things?') when used as a greeting, requires a simple formula response, such as 'Fine'; it is often reduced to **pen ŋay bâaŋ** or **pen ŋay**:

pen yaŋŋay bâaŋ?

เป็นอย่างไรบ้าง

How are things?

– **sabaay dii khráp/khâ**

– สบายดีครับ/ค่ะ

– Fine.

How/what about . . .? questions

How/What about . . .? is used as a non-initiating question when the topic of conversation is defined and the kind of information to be supplied is understood by both parties; it is formed by the pattern: **lɛ́ɛw +
NOUN + lâ?**:

lɛ́ɛw khun lâ?

แล้วคุณล่ะ

And how/what about you?

lɛ́ɛw phɯ̂an lâ?

แล้วเพื่อนล่ะ

And how/what about your friend?

lɛ́ɛw phrûŋ níi lâ?

แล้วพรุ่งนี้ล่ะ

And how/what about tomorrow?

12.3   Alternative questions

Alternative questions (Do you want tea *or* coffee?) link two phrases with **rɯ̌ɯ** ('or') which in spoken Thai is normally pronounced **rɯ́**:

pay duu nǎŋ rɯ́ klàp bâan?

ไปดูหนังหรือกลับบ้าน

Shall we see a film or go home?

aw nám chaa rɤ́ kaafɛɛ?
เอาน้ำชาหรือกาแฟ
Do you want tea or coffee?

To reply to such questions, you repeat the appropriate phrase, e.g. **klàp bâan** 'Go home'; **aw kaafɛɛ** ('I'll have coffee').

A much-contracted form of alternative question common in spoken Thai is formed by VERB + **mây** + VERB:

pay mây pay?
ไปไม่ไป
Are you going or not? (lit. go – not – go)

sɤ́ɤ mây sɤ́ɤ?
ซื้อไม่ซื้อ
Are you going to buy it or not? (lit. buy – not – buy)

These could be expanded using **rɤ́** to **ca pay rɤ́ ca mây pay?** (will – go – or – will – not – go) and **ca sɤ́ɤ rɤ́ ca mây sɤ́ɤ?** (will – buy – or – will – not – buy).

12.4 Indirect questions

Indirect questions are formed by the pattern: SUBJECT + **thǎam** ('to ask') + (DIRECT OBJECT) + **wâa** ('that') + DIRECT QUESTION:

Direct question
ca klàp khɯɯn níi máy?
จะกลับคืนนี้ไหม
Will you be back tonight?

Indirect question
kháw thǎam wâa ca klàp khɯɯn níi máy?
เขาถามว่าจะกลับคืนนี้ไหม
He asked if I'd be back tonight.

Direct question
mii fɛɛn rɤ́ yaŋ?
มีแฟนหรือยัง
Do you have a boyfriend?

Indirect question
phǒm thǎam kháw wâa mii fɛɛn rɤ́ yaŋ?
ผมถามเขาว่ามีแฟนหรือยัง
I asked her if she had a boyfriend.

For indirect speech, see 5.9, 9.3.

Chapter 13

Numbers, measurement and quantification

The most common word for 'number' in Thai is **lêek**. It is commonly followed by **thîi** in expressions like 'number nine', 'house number 38' and so on. It is also often prefixed by **mǎay**. The word **bəə**, from English 'number', has a more restricted usage, most commonly with telephone numbers and room numbers. **camnuan** means 'number' in the sense of 'quantity' or in expressions like 'a number of my friends'.

lêek faràŋ	เลขฝรั่ง	Arabic numbers
lêek thay	เลขไทย	Thai numbers
lêek khûu	เลขคู่	even number
lêek khîi	เลขคี่	odd number
lêek thîi kâaw	เลขที่เก้า	number nine
bâan lêek thîi cèt	บ้านเลขที่เจ็ด	house no. 7
mǎay lêek thîi sìp	หมายเลขที่สิบ	number ten

hɔ̂ŋ bəə yîi sìp sǎam
ห้องเบอร์ยี่สิบสาม
room no. 23

bəə thoorasàp
เบอร์โทรศัพท์
telephone number

phɯ̂an camnuan nɯ̀ŋ
เพื่อนจำนวนหนึ่ง
a number of friends

13.1 Cardinal numbers

Both Thai and Arabic numbers are in common everyday use. Thai script numerals are identical to those found in the Cambodian script, while the Lao script employs some but not all of the same number symbols.

0	**sǔun**	ศูนย์	๐
1	**nèŋ**	หนึ่ง	๑
2	**sɔ̌ɔŋ**	สอง	๒
3	**sǎam**	สาม	๓
4	**sìi**	สี่	๔
5	**hâa**	ห้า	๕
6	**hòk**	หก	๖
7	**cèt**	เจ็ด	๗
8	**pɛ̀ɛt**	แปด	๘
9	**kâaw**	เก้า	๙
10	**sìp**	สิบ	๑๐

Numbers 12–19 are formed regularly using **sìp** + UNIT; eleven is irregular, using **èt** instead of **nèŋ**:

11	**sìp èt**	สิบเอ็ด	๑๑
12	**sìp sɔ̌ɔŋ**	สิบสอง	๑๒
13	**sìp sǎam**	สิบสาม	๑๓
14	**sìp sìi**	สิบสี่	๑๔

Multiples of 10 up to 90 use **sìp** ('ten') as a suffix and are regular with the exception of 'twenty', which uses **yîi** instead of **sɔ̌ɔŋ**:

20	**yîi sìp**	ยี่สิบ	๒๐
30	**sǎam sìp**	สามสิบ	๓๐
40	**sìi sìp**	สี่สิบ	๔๐
50	**hâa sìp**	ห้าสิบ	๕๐
60	**hòk sìp**	หกสิบ	๖๐

70	cèt sìp	เจ็ดสิบ	๗๐
80	pὲὲt sìp	แปดสิบ	๘๐
90	kâaw sìp	เก้าสิบ	๙๐

Numbers between 10 and 100 are formed in a regular way with the exception of 21, 31, 41, etc. where the word for 'one' is èt and not nừŋ. In numbers 21–29, yîi sìp is often contracted to yîip in informal spoken Thai:

21	yîi sìp èt (yîip èt)	ยี่สิบเอ็ด	๒๑
22	yîi sìp sɔ̌ɔŋ (yîip sɔ̌ɔŋ)	ยี่สิบสอง	๒๒
23	yîi sìp sǎam (yîip sǎam)	ยี่สิบสาม	๒๓
31	sǎam sìp èt	สามสิบเอ็ด	๓๑
32	sǎam sìp sɔ̌ɔŋ	สามสิบสอง	๓๒
33	sǎam sìp sǎam	สามสิบสาม	๓๓
41	sìi sìp èt	สี่สิบเอ็ด	๔๑
42	sìi sìp sɔ̌ɔŋ	สี่สิบสอง	๔๒
51	hâa sìp èt	ห้าสิบเอ็ด	๕๑

Numbers from 100 upwards are also formed regularly, but in addition to words for 'thousand' and 'million', there are also specific words for 'ten thousand' (mừừn) and 'hundred thousand' (sɛ̌ɛn):

100	(nừŋ) rɔ́ɔy	(หนึ่ง) ร้อย
101	(nừŋ) rɔ́ɔy èt	(หนึ่ง) ร้อยเอ็ด
102	(nừŋ) rɔ́ɔy sɔ̌ɔŋ	(หนึ่ง) ร้อยสอง
1000	(nừŋ) phan	(หนึ่ง) พัน
1002	(nừŋ) phan (kàp) sɔ̌ɔŋ	(หนึ่ง) พัน(กับ)สอง
1200	(nừŋ) phan sɔ̌ɔŋ (rɔ́ɔy)	(หนึ่ง) พันสอง(ร้อย)
10,000	(nừŋ) mừừn	(หนึ่ง) หมื่น
100,000	(nừŋ) sɛ̌ɛn	(หนึ่ง) แสน
1,000,000	(nừŋ) láan	(หนึ่ง) ล้าน

Numbers, including the year, are read as in the following examples; years may be prefaced by **pii** ('year'):

1986	**(pii) nὺŋ phan kâaw rɔ́ɔy pὲɛt sìp hòk**
2541	**(pii) sɔ̌ɔŋ phan hâa rɔ́ɔy sìi sìp èt**
75,862	**cèt mὺɯn hâa phan pὲɛt rɔ́ɔy hòk sìp sɔ̌ɔŋ**
432,925	**sìi sɛ̌ɛn sǎam mὺɯn sɔ̌ɔŋ phan kâaw rɔ́ɔy yîi sìp hâa**

When a cardinal number occurs with a noun, the appropriate classifier must also be used (3.5.1, 3.5.5, 3.5.8).

13.2 Cardinal numbers with *sàk* and *tâŋ*

sàk + CARDINAL NUMBER + CLASSIFIER conveys the sense of 'as little/ few as', 'merely' or 'just', and is often reinforced by **thâwnán** ('only') at the end of the phrase; sometimes it simply conveys the idea of approximation. When **sàk** occurs before a classifier with no number word, it is understood that 'one' has been omitted:

phǒm pay sàk hâa wan
ผมไปสักห้าวัน
I'm going for five days, or so.

raw khuy kan sàk chûamooŋ thâwnán
เราคุยกันสักชั่วโมงเท่านั้น
We chatted for just an hour.

raw yàak mii lûuk sàk khon sɔ̌ɔŋ khon
เราอยากมีลูกสักคนสองคน
We'd like to have a child or two.

tâŋ + CARDINAL NUMBER + CLASSIFIER conveys the idea of 'as much/many as':

kháw khuy kan tâŋ sǎam chûamooŋ
เขาคุยกันตั้งสามชั่วโมง
They chatted for as long as three hours.

kháw rian tâŋ hâa pii lɛ́ɛw
เขาเรียนตั้งห้าปีแล้ว
He has studied for as long as five years.

Both sàk and tâŋ can be used with other, non-numerical quantifier words such as 'a little' and 'a long time':

rɔɔ ìik sàk nɔ̀y dâay máy?
รออีกสักหน่อยได้ไหม
Can you wait a little longer?

phŏm mây dây phóp kháw tâŋ naan
ผมไม่ได้พบเขาตั้งนาน
I haven't met him for a long time.

13.3 Ordinal numbers

Ordinal numbers in Thai are formed by the pattern, thîi + CARDINAL NUMBER:

thîi nɨ̀ŋ	ที่หนึ่ง	first
thîi sɔ̌ɔŋ	ที่สอง	second
thîi sǎam	ที่สาม	third

When an ordinal number occurs with a noun, the appropriate classifier must also be used (3.5.3, 3.5.9).

The word rɛ̂ɛk also means 'first', but in a historical sense rather than in rank order. It is therefore not always interchangeable with thîi nɨ̀ŋ:

khráŋ thîi nɨ̀ŋ/khráŋ rɛ̂ɛk
ครั้งที่หนึ่ง/ครั้งแรก
the first time

But:

raaŋwan thîi nɨ̀ŋ
รางวัลที่หนึ่ง
the first (top) prize

raaŋwan (khráŋ) rɛ̂ɛk
รางวัล(ครั้ง)แรก
the inaugural prize

Note that in the expression thii rɛ̂ɛk ('at first'), the word thii ('time') is a noun, pronounced with a mid-tone, not the location marker thîi ('at'):

thii rɛ̂ɛk ɕhán mây ɕhɔ̂ɔp kháw
ทีแรกฉันไม่ชอบเขา
At first I didn't like him.

'Firstly', 'secondly', and so on, used in putting forward numbered points in a reasoned argument, follow the pattern **prakaan** ('item, sort, kind') + ORDINAL NUMBER:

prakaan thîi nừŋ	ประการที่หนึ่ง	firstly
or		
prakaan rɛ̂ɛk	ประการแรก	
prakaan thîi sɔ̌ɔŋ	ประการที่สอง	secondly
prakaan thîi sǎam	ประการที่สาม	thirdly

13.4 Sanskrit numbers

The Sanskrit numbers **èek** ('one'), **thoo** ('two') and **trii** ('three') are used with academic degrees and military ranks, and in the names of tones and tone marks (2.5.2):

parinyaa èek/thoo/trii
ปริญญาเอก/โท/ตรี
PhD/MA, MSc, etc./BA, BSc, etc.

phon (tamrùat) èek/thoo/trii
พล(ตำรวจ)เอก/โท/ตรี
(police) general/lieutenant-general/major-general

The word **thoo** is also used instead of **sɔ̌ɔŋ** when giving telephone numbers, which are read as if each unit is a single digit:

bəə thoorasàp thoo sìi hâa – sǎam thoo kâaw pὲὲt
telephone number, two four five – three two nine eight

Other Sanskrit numbers appear in the words for 'decade', 'decathlon' and 'century':

thótsawát	ทศวรรษ	decade
thótsakriithaa	ทศกรีฑา	decathlon
sàtawát	ศตวรรษ	century

13.5 Once, twice . . .

'Once', 'twice', and so on, are formed using CARDINAL NUMBER + khráŋ or hǒn, both of which mean 'time' or 'occasion':

nʉ̀ŋ khráŋ/hǒn	หนึ่งครั้ง/หน	once, one time
sɔ̌ɔŋ khráŋ	สองครั้ง	twice
sǎam khráŋ	สามครั้ง	three times

nʉ̀ŋ when it occurs after khráŋ is less emphatic; diaw ('single') may be used after khráŋ, instead of nʉ̀ŋ, for greater emphasis:

| khráŋ nʉ̀ŋ | ครั้งหนึ่ง | once, on one occasion |
| khráŋ diaw | ครั้งเดียว | (just) once, on a single occasion |

khráŋ and hǒn are also used with ordinal numbers to mean 'first time', 'second time', and so on:

khráŋ thîi nʉ̀ŋ	ครั้งที่หนึ่ง	the first time
or		
khráŋ rɛ̂ɛk	ครั้งแรก	
khráŋ thîi sɔ̌ɔŋ	ครั้งที่สอง	the second time
khráŋ thîi sǎam	ครั้งที่สาม	the third time

13.6 Fractions, decimals, percentages, multiples

13.6.1 Fractions

Fractions, other than 'half', are expressed by the pattern sèet ('numerator') + NUMBER + sùan ('denominator') + NUMBER:

| sèet nʉ̀ŋ sùan sìi | เศษหนึ่งส่วนสี่ | quarter |
| sèet sǎam sùan sìi | เศษสามส่วนสี่ | three-quarters |

However, in expressions like 'three-quarters of the population . . .', sǎam nay sìi (three – in – four) is more common:

prachaachon sǎam nay sìi
ประชาชนสามในสี่
three-quarters of the population

khrûŋ ('half') behaves like other number words in occurring after a noun and before a classifier:

lâw khrûŋ khùat
เหล้าครึ่งขวด
half a bottle of whisky

khrûŋ wan
ครึ่งวัน
half a day

khrûŋ ('half') also occurs after a classifier in the pattern NOUN + (NUMBER +) CLASSIFIER + khrûŋ to mean 'NUMBER and a half'; if no number word appears, the phrase conveys the idea of 'one and a half':

lâw sɔ̌ɔŋ khùat khrûŋ
เหล้าสองขวดครึ่ง
two and a half bottles of whisky

raw pay dʉan khrûŋ
เราไปเดือนครึ่ง
We went for a month and a half.

13.6.2 Decimals

Decimal numbers are read as NUMBER + cùt ('point') + NUMBER; decimals behave like other numbers in being followed by a classifier:

sìi cùt hâa
สี่จุดห้า
4.5

yaaw hòk cùt hâa sǎam níw
ยาวหกจุดห้าสามนิ้ว
6.53 inches long

13.6.3 Percentages

The word pəəsen ('per cent') is borrowed directly from English. It is used in the pattern, NOUN + NUMBER + pəəsen; in sentences, the verb may occur immediately after the noun or after pəəsen:

prachaachon sìp cùt hâa pəəsen
ประชาชนสิบจุดห้าเปอร์เซ็นต์
10.5 per cent of the people

nák sÿksăa sɔ̀ɔp tòk săam sìp pəəsen
นักศึกษาสอบตกสามสิบเปอร์เซนต์
Thirty per cent of the students failed.

Percentages may also be expressed by the pattern, NOUN + rɔ́ɔy la ('per hundred') + NUMBER + CLASSIFIER, although this is now less common than pəəsen.

13.6.4 *Multiples*

'X times more . . .' is expressed by the pattern ADJECTIVE/ ADVERB + kwàa + NUMBER + thâw:

yày kwàa săam thâw
ใหญ่กว่าสามเท่า
three times bigger

sanùk kwàa phan thâw
สนุกกว่าพันเท่า
a thousand times more fun

13.7 Collective numbers

The collective numbers khûu ('pair') and lŏo ('dozen') behave like classifiers and occur in the pattern NOUN + NUMBER + COLLECTIVE NUMBER:

rɔɔŋ tháaw̤ săam khûu
รองเท้าสามคู่
three pairs of shoes

khày khrÿ̂ŋ lŏo
ไข่ครึ่งโหล
half a dozen eggs

13.8 Some idiomatic expressions involving numbers

sɛ̌ɛn ('one hundred thousand') or sɛ̌ɛn ca or sɛ̌ɛn thîi ca is used before
a verb/adjective to mean 'extremely', 'ever so . . .':

sɛ̌ɛn klay
แสนไกล
extremely far

sɛ̌ɛn ca sanùk
แสนจะสนุก
ever such fun

rɔ́ɔy pɛ̀ɛt ('one hundred and eight') means 'all kinds of'; it is sometimes
further intensified by the addition of **phan** ('thousand'):

panhǎa rɔ́ɔy pɛ̀ɛt (phan) prakaan
ปัญหาร้อยแปด(พัน)ประการ
all kinds of problems

hâa rɔ́ɔy ('five hundred'), curiously, is added to the word **coon** ('bandit,
thief') but to no other noun; it does not indicate plurality, nor intensify
the scale of thievery, nor reflect the speaker's attitude:

coon hâa rɔ́ɔy
โจรห้าร้อย
bandit, thief

sǎam sìp sɔ̌ɔŋ ('thirty-two') is used with the word **aakaan** ('state, condition, sign') in the expression **aakaan khróp sǎam sìp sɔ̌ɔŋ** ('to be perfectly
normal'). Literally, it means 'the full thirty-two conditions' and is a reference to the traditional belief that the body comprised thirty-two integral
parts, including hair, teeth, skin, fingernails, limbs and internal organs.
The expression is used to describe newly born children or those escaping
injury in an accident.

aakaan khróp sǎam sìp sɔ̌ɔŋ
อาการครบสามสิบสอง
to be perfectly normal

kâaw ('nine') is regarded as lucky because it is identical in pronunciation
(but not spelling) to a part of the word for 'to progress' (**kâaw nâa**):

kâaw	เก้า	nine
kâaw nâa	ก้าวหน้า	to progress

13.9 Measurements

Measurements, such as 'three metres *wide*', 'two hours *long*' and 'six feet *tall*' follow the pattern TYPE OF MEASUREMENT (i.e. length, weight, etc.) + NUMBER + UNIT OF MEASUREMENT:

yaaw cèt níw
ยาวเจ็ดนิ้ว
seven inches long

nàk hâa sìp kiloo
หนักห้าสิบกิโล
fifty kilos in weight

Area is expressed as NUMBER + **taraaŋ** ('square') + UNIT OF MEASURE-MENT:

sìp taraaŋ méet
สิบตารางเมตร
ten square metres

Plots of land are normally measured in **taraaŋ waa** (square *waa*; 1 sq. *waa* = 4 sq. metres) or **rây** (*rai*; 1 *rai* = 1600 sq. metres or 400 square *waa*; 2.53 *rai* = 1 acre). Note that **waa** is a linear measurement and is therefore preceded by **taraaŋ**, but **rây** is itself an area measurement and thus does not occur with **taraaŋ**:

sìi sìp taraaŋ waa
สี่สิบตารางวา
forty square *waa*

sìp rây
สิบไร่
ten *rai*

13.10 Distances

The distance between two places can be expressed by the pattern PLACE A + **yùu** ('to be located') + **klay càak** ('far from') + PLACE B + NUMBER + UNIT OF MEASUREMENT:

hǔa hǐn yùu klay càak kruŋthêep sɔ̌ɔŋ rɔ́ɔy kiloomét
หัวหินอยู่ไกลจากกรุงเทพฯ ๒๐๐ กิโลเมตร
Hua Hin is 200 kilometres from Bangkok.

hàaŋ càak ('far from') can be used as an alternative to klay càak:

praysanii yùu hàaŋ càak bâan mây kìi naathii
ไปรษณีย์อยู่ห่างจากบ้านไม่กี่นาที
The post office is a few minutes from my house.

13.11 Distribution: 'per'

Expressions like '500 baht per person', 'six times per week' and '50 baht a kilo' involve the use of la ('per'); the word order in Thai is the opposite to English (e.g. person – per – 500 baht), with the number expression occuring after la:

khon la hâa rɔ́ɔy bàat
คนละห้าร้อยบาท
500 baht per person

aathít la hòk khráŋ
อาทิตย์ละหกครั้ง
six times a week

loo la hâa sìp bàat
โลละห้าสิบบาท
50 baht a kilo

Note the idiomatic expressions **khon la rûaŋ** ('a different matter') and **khon la yàaŋ** ('a different type'), where **khon** does not mean 'person':

pen khon la rûaŋ
เป็นคนละเรื่อง
That's a different matter.

nîi pen khon la yàaŋ
นี่เป็นคนละอย่าง
This is a different kind.

13.12 Quantifiers

The following quantifiers occur in the pattern (NOUN +) QUANTIFIER + CLASSIFIER (3.5.2). They occupy the same position between nouns and classifiers as cardinal numbers (3.5.1) and can therefore be thought of as 'number words'. All, with the exception of **mâak**, can occur before a classifier without a preceding noun:

thúk	ทุก	every, all
tὲὲ la	แต่ละ	each
baaŋ	บาง	some
lăay	หลาย	several, many
mây kìi	ไม่กี่	not many
nɔ́ɔy	น้อย	few
mâak	มาก	many

chûaŋ weelaa lăay dʉan
ช่วงเวลาหลายเดือน
a period of several/many months

aahăan baaŋ yàaŋ
อาหารบางอย่าง
some kinds of food

In phrases involving **nɔ́ɔy** ('few'), the classifier is commonly omitted, while in phrases involving **mâak** ('many'), the classifier is normally omitted:

kháw mii phʉ̂an nɔ́ɔy (khon)
เขามีเพื่อนน้อย(คน)
He has few friends.

nay sà náam mii plaa mâak (tua)
ในสระน้ำมีปลามาก(ตัว)
In the pond there are many fish.

A small number of quantifiers, including **yə́** ('many'), **yέ** ('many'), **yə́yέ** ('many'), **mâakmaay** ('many'), **nítnɔ̀y** ('a little'), **léknɔ́ɔy** ('few, little'), follow a noun, but do not occur with classifiers; because **mâak** only occurs with a classifier in rather stylised Thai, it can be included with this group:

kháw mii fεεn yə́/yέ/yə́ yέ/mâakmaay/mâak
เขามีแฟนแยอะ/แยะ/เยอะแยะ/มากมาย/มาก
She's got lots of boyfriends.

sày nám taan nítnɔ̀y
ใส่น้ำตาลนิดหน่อย
Put a little sugar in.

mii aahăan lʉ̆a léknɔ́ɔy
มีอาหารเหลือเล็กน้อย
There's a little food left over.

The quantifiers **mâak** and **nítnɔ̀y** also function as adverbs of degree; the similarity in both sound and meaning between the quantifier **baaŋ** and the adverb of degree **bâaŋ** is often confusing for the learner (7.6).

13.13   Negative quantification

Negative quantities (e.g. no brothers and sisters, there isn't any fish sauce) are expressed by the pattern **mây mii** ('there are not') + NOUN:

mây mii phîi nɔ́ɔŋ
ไม่มีพี่น้อง
no brothers and sisters

mây mii nám plaa
ไม่มีน้ำปลา
There's no fish sauce.

13.14   Approximation: 'about'

Approximation is expressed using **pramaan** or **raaw** (both of which mean 'about') + NUMBER + CLASSIFIER:

nák thɔ̂ŋ thîaw pramaan rɔ́ɔy khon
นักท่องเที่ยวประมาณร้อยคน
about 100 tourists

raaw hòk chûamooŋ
ราวหกชั่วโมง
about six hours

Two consecutive numbers also convey approximation:

sɔ̌ɔŋ sǎam wan
สองสามวัน
two or three days

hâa hòk khon
ห้าหกคน
five or six people

A range of numbers (from . . . to . . .) is expressed by NUMBER + **thǔŋ** ('to') + NUMBER + CLASSIFIER:

sìp thʉ̌ŋ sìp hâa khon
สิบถึงสิบห้าคน
(from) ten to fifteen people

Lower limits can be expressed by **yàaŋ nɔ́ɔy thîi sut** ('at least') + NUMBER + CLASSIFIER:

yàaŋ nɔ́ɔy thîi sùt sǎam wan
อย่างน้อยที่สุดสามวัน
at least three days

Upper limits ('at the most') follow a similar pattern using **mâak** ('much') instead of **nɔ́ɔy**:

yàaŋ mâak thîi sùt mʉ̀ʉn bàat
อย่างมากที่สุดหมื่นบาท
at the most 10,000 baht

13.15 Restriction: 'only'

There are several different words for 'only ...' and they can occur in various combinations:

a   NOUN + NUMBER + CLASSIFIER + **thâwnán**
b   NOUN + **phiaŋ** + NUMBER + CLASSIFIER (+ **thâwnán**)
c   NOUN + (**phiaŋ**) + **tɛ̀ɛ** + NUMBER + CLASSIFIER (+ **thâwnán**)
d   NOUN + (**phiaŋ**) + **khɛ̂ɛ** + NUMBER + CLASSIFIER (+ **thâwnán**)

Note, however, that the order, NUMBER + CLASSIFIER is normally reversed when the number is 'one' (see 3.5.1) and the word **diaw** ('single') is commonly used instead of **nʉ̀ŋ** ('one'). The use of **tɛ̀ɛ** ('but') to mean 'only' is mirrored in the archaic English usage of 'but' in statements like 'I have but three daughters fair.'

kháw mii lûuk sɔ̌ɔŋ khon thâwnán
เขามีลูกสองคนเท่านั้น
They have only two children.

phǒm ca kin bia khùat diaw thâwnán
ผมจะกินเบียร์ขวดเดียวเท่านั้น
I'll have only one beer.

ŋən lɤ̌a phiaŋ sìi rɔ́ɔy bàat (thâwnán)

เงินเหลือเพียงสี่ร้อยบาท(เท่านั้น)

There is only four hundred baht left.

mii faràŋ tɛ̀ɛ sɔ̌ɔŋ khon (thâwnán)

มีฝรั่งแต่สองคน(เท่านั้น)

There were only two Westerners.

chán pay thîaw chiaŋmày khɛ̂ɛ sǎam wan (thâwnán)

ฉันไปเที่ยวเชียงใหม่แค่สามวัน(เท่านั้น)

I went to Chiangmai for only three days.

13.16 'More than'

'More than . . .' is usually expressed using the word **kwàa** ('more than,
-er than'); its position in relation to the number and classifier varies.

13.16.1 NOUN + NUMBER + kwàa + CLASSIFIER

This pattern tends to be used when dealing with multiples of ten and
round numbers:

kháw sú́ɯ sɯ̂a rɔ́ɔy kwàa tua

เขาซื้อเสื้อร้อยกว่าตัว

She bought more than 100 blouses.

chán dây ŋən dɯan sɔ̌ɔŋ mɯ̀ɯn kwàa bàat

ฉันได้เงินเดือนสองหมื่นกว่าบาท

I get a monthly salary of more than 20,000 baht.

raw dəən thaaŋ yîi sìp kwàa chûamooŋ

เราเดินทางยี่สิบกว่าชั่วโมง

We travelled for more than twenty hours.

13.16.2 NOUN + kwàa + NUMBER + CLASSIFIER

This pattern is also used only with large round numbers:

mii tamrùat kwàa rɔ́ɔy khon

มีตำรวจกว่าร้อยคน

There were more than 100 policemen.

13.16.3 NOUN + mâak kwàa + NUMBER + CLASSIFIER

This pattern can be used generally and with non-round numbers:

nǎŋsǔu mâak kwàa sìp hâa lêm
หนังสือมากกว่าสิบห้าเล่ม
more than fifteen books

kháw kin bia mâak kwàa hòk khùat
เขากินเบียร์มากกว่าหกขวด
He drank more than six bottles of beer.

mâak kwàa can be substituted by either kəən ('in excess of') or kəən kwàa:

nák rian kəən (kwàa) sǎam sìp hâa khon
นักเรียนเกิน(กว่า)สามสิบห้าคน
more than thirty pupils

13.16.4 NOUN + NUMBER + CLASSIFIER + kwàa

This pattern is used to convey the idea of a fraction – but not a whole unit – more; kwàa is sometimes reduplicated, with the first element pronounced with a mid-tone and a shortened vowel:

chán rɔɔ sɔ̌ɔŋ chûamooŋ kwàa
ฉันรอสองชั่วโมงกว่า
I waited over two hours.

bàay sìi mooŋ kwa kwàa
บ่ายสี่โมงกว่าๆ
a little after 4 p.m.

Note the difference between

kháw kin bia sɔ̌ɔŋ khùat kwàa
เขากินเบียร์สองขวดกว่า
He has drunk over two bottles of beer (but not as many as three).

and

kháw kin bia mâak kwàa sɔ̌ɔŋ khùat
เขากินเบียร์มากกว่าสองขวด
He has drunk more than two bottles of beer (i.e. at least three).

13.17 'Less than'

'Less than . . .' can be expressed most simply by the pattern (NOUN) + nɔ́ɔy kwàa ('less than') + NUMBER + CLASSIFIER:

phûu yày nɔ́ɔy kwàa sìp khon
ผู้ใหญ่น้อยกว่าสิบคน
less than ten adults

kháw phûut nɔ́ɔy kwàa hâa naathii
เขาพูดน้อยกว่าห้านาที
He spoke for less than five minutes.

The negative form of the 'as many as' construction (13.18), NOUN + mây thɯ̌ŋ + NUMBER + CLASSIFIER, is also commonly used to express 'less than':

kháw dây ŋen dɯan mây thɯ̌ŋ mɯ̀ɯn bàat
เขาได้เงินเดือนไม่ถึงหมื่นบาท
He gets a monthly salary of less than 10,000 baht.

13.18 'As many as'

'As many as . . .' or 'up to . . .' is expressed by the pattern NOUN + thɯ̌ŋ ('to reach') + NUMBER + CLASSIFIER:

mii khon samàk thɯ̌ŋ phan khon
มีคนสมัครถึงพันคน
There were as many as a thousand applicants.

For the negative form, see 13.17.

Chapter 14

Time

14.1 Days

Days of the week are normally prefaced by the word **wan** ('day'); no preposition, corresponding to English 'on', is used:

Monday	**wan can**	วันจันทร์
Tuesday	**wan aŋkhaan**	วันอังคาร
Wednesday	**wan phút**	วันพุธ
Thursday	**wan phартhàt**	วันพฤหัส*
Friday	**wan sùk**	วันศุกร์
Saturday	**wan săaw**	วันเสาร์
Sunday	**wan aathít**	วันอาทิตย์

raw ca klàp wan phút
เราจะกลับวันพุธ
We shall return on Wednesday.

*Note the alternative, very formal pronunciation:

wan phартhàtsabɔɔdii   วันพฤหัสบดี

14.2 Parts of the day

Words like **cháaw** ('morning') and **bàay** ('afternoon') may optionally be prefixed with the word **tɔɔn** ('a period of time') to express the idea 'in the morning', 'in the afternoon', etc.:

| morning | **(tɔɔn) cháaw** | (ตอน)เช้า |
| noon | **(tɔɔn) thîaŋ (wan)** | (ตอน)เที่ยงวัน |

189

afternoon	**(tɔɔn) bàay**	(ตอน)บ่าย
(early) evening	**(tɔɔn) yen**	(ตอน)เย็น
night time	**(tɔɔn) klaaŋ khʉʉn**	(ตอน)กลางคืน
daytime	**(tɔɔn) klaaŋ wan**	(ตอน)กลางวัน

pay cháaw klap yen
ไปเช้ากลับเย็น
We'll go in the morning and return in the evening.

tɔɔn bàay chán mây wâaŋ
ตอนบ่ายฉันไม่ว่าง
I'm not free in the afternoon.

14.3 Months

Months with 31 days end in -khom, those with 30 days in -yon and February ends in -phan. In normal speech, the word **dʉan** ('month') is often prefixed and the final syllable omitted; no preposition corresponding to English 'in' is used:

January	**mókkaraakhom**	มกราคม
February	**kumphaaphan**	กุมภาพันธ์
March	**miinaakhom**	มีนาคม
April	**meesǎayon**	เมษายน
May	**phrʉ́tsaphaakhom**	พฤษภาคม
June	**míthunaayon**	มิถุนายน
July	**karákkadaakhom**	กรกฎาคม
August	**sǐŋhǎakhom**	สิงหาคม
September	**kanyaayon**	กันยายน
October	**tulaakhom**	ตุลาคม
November	**phrʉ́tsacìkkaayon**	พฤศจิกายน
December	**thanwaakhom**	ธันวาคม

kháw pay dʉan sǐŋhǎa
เขาไปเดือนสิงหาฯ
He's going in August.

Years

The year is calculated according to the Buddhist Era (B.E.) (**phút-thasàkkaràat**, or **phɔɔ sɔ̆ɔ** for short) which dates from the birth of the Buddha, 543 years before the birth of Christ. To convert Thai years to AD (**khríttasàkkaràat**, or **khɔɔ sɔ̆ɔ** for short), subtract 543; thus, 2500 B.E is 1957 AD, while 2000 AD is 2543 B.E.

To express the idea that something happened or will happen in a certain year, the word **pii** ('year') is used before the number; the preposition **nay** ('in') may preface **pii** but this is more common in formal written Thai than in the spoken language:

kháw tɛ̀ŋ ŋaan (nay) pii sɔ̆ɔŋ phan hâa rɔ́ɔy yîi sìp èt
เขาแต่งงาน(ใน)ปี ๒๕๒๑
He got married in 2521 (1978).

Most Thais are also aware of their birth year in the twelve-year cycle in which each year is named after an animal. This animal term is specific to the year and is not used to refer to the living creature. The animal year is normally prefaced by the word **pii**:

Year of the Rat (1948, 1960 . . .)	**pii chûat**	ปีชวด
Year of the Ox (1949, 1961 . . .)	**pii chalŭu**	ปีฉลู
Year of the Tiger (1950, 1962 . . .)	**pii khăan**	ปีขาล
Year of the Rabbit (1951, 1963 . . .)	**pii thɔ̀**	ปีเถาะ
Year of the Dragon (1952, 1964 . . .)	**pii marooŋ**	ปีมะโรง
Year of the Snake (1953, 1965 . . .)	**pii masɛ̆ŋ**	ปีมะเส็ง
Year of the Horse (1954, 1966 . . .)	**pii mamia**	ปีมะเมีย
Year of the Goat (1955, 1967 . . .)	**pii mamɛɛ**	ปีมะแม
Year of the Monkey (1956, 1968 . . .)	**pii wɔ̂ɔk**	ปีวอก
Year of the Cock (1957, 1969 . . .)	**pii rakaa**	ปีระกา
Year of the Dog (1958, 1970 . . .)	**pii cɔɔ**	ปีจอ
Year of the Pig (1959, 1971 . . .)	**pii kun**	ปีกุน

A twelve-year cycle is called **rɔ̂ɔp pii**; the 'completion of five cycles' (**khróp hâa rɔ̂ɔp**), that is the sixtieth birthday, is traditionally celebrated as a major milestone in a person's life.

In addition to the Western New Year (**pii mày,**) both the traditional Thai New Year (**sǒŋkraan**), which occurs on 13 April, and the Chinese New Year (**trùt ciin**), in February, are widely celebrated. Thailand adopted the international convention of beginning the new year on 1 January in 1941.

14.5 Dates

Dates are expressed using the pattern **wan** ('day') + ORDINAL NUMBER + MONTH (+ YEAR):

wan thîi sìp sìi tulaa (sǒɔŋ phan hâa rɔ́ɔy sìp hòk)
วันที่ ๑๔ ตุลาฯ (๒๕๑๖)
14 October (2516)

'What date . . .?' questions use the expression, **wan thîi thâwrày?**:

wan níi (pen) wan thîi thâwrày?
วันนี้(เป็น)วันที่เท่าไร
What is the date today?

pay wan thîi thâwrày?
ไปวันที่เท่าไร
What date are you going?

14.6 Seasons

There are three seasons in Thailand, the cool season (November to February), the hot season (March to June) and the rainy season (July to October). The formal Thai word for 'season' is **rúduu** but **nâa** is more commonly used in speech. 'Spring/autumn' literally translate as 'season – leaves – burst forth/fall'.

cool season	**nâa (rúduu) nǎaw**	หน้า (ฤดู) หนาว
hot season	**nâa rɔ́ɔn**	หน้าร้อน
rainy season	**nâa fǒn**	หน้าฝน
spring	**nâa bay máay plì**	หน้าใบไม้ผลิ
autumn	**nâa bay máay rûaŋ**	หน้าใบไม้ร่วง

14.7 Useful expressions of time

In this section common expressions of time are listed at some length because of some unpredictable irregularities in the patterns. The word **mûa** occurs in expressions of past time; where it appears in brackets, it is optional.

14.7.1 'Today', 'tomorrow', 'yesterday'

today	**wan níi**	วันนี้
tomorrow	**phrûŋ níi**	พรุ่งนี้
the day after tomorrow	**marʉʉn**	มะรืน
yesterday	**mûa waan (níi)**	เมื่อวาน(นี้)
the day before yesterday	**mûa waan sʉʉn(níi)**	เมื่อวานซืน(นี้)
this morning	**cháaw níi**	เช้านี้
this afternoon	**bàay níi**	บ่ายนี้
this evening	**yen níi**	เย็นนี้
tonight	**khʉʉn níi**	คืนนี้
yesterday morning	**cháaw (mûa) waan**	เช้า(เมื่อ)วาน
yesterday afternoon	**bàay (mûa) waan**	บ่าย(เมื่อ)วาน
yesterday evening	**yen (mûa) waan**	เย็น(เมื่อ)วาน
yesterday night	**mûa khʉʉn**	เมื่อคืน
tomorrow morning	**phrûŋ níi cháaw**	พรุ่งนี้เช้า
tomorrow afternoon	**phrûŋ níi bàay**	พรุ่งนี้บ่าย
tomorrow evening	**phrûŋ níi yen**	พรุ่งนี้เย็น
tomorrow night	**khʉʉn phrûŋ níi**	คืนพรุ่งนี้

'This', 'next', 'last . . .'

The words **níi** ('this'), **nâa** ('next') and **thîi lɛ́ɛw** ('last') can occur after
any unit of time. (**mʉ̂a**) . . . may optionally be used with **thîi lɛ́ɛw** in 'last
week/month/year'. **pii klaay** and (**wan**) **rûŋ khʉ̂n** are fixed expressions:

this week	**aathít níi**	อาทิตย์นี้
next month	**dʉan nâa**	เดือนหน้า
last year	**(mʉ̂a) pii thîi lɛ́ɛw**	(เมื่อ)ปีที่แล้ว
last year	**pii klaay**	ปีกลาย
the next day	**(wan) rûŋ khʉ̂n**	(วัน)รุ่งขึ้น

14.7.3 **'Beginning', 'during', 'middle', 'end'**

14.7.3.1 'Beginning': **tôn**

tôn pii thîi lɛ́ɛw
ต้นปีที่แล้ว
the beginning of last year

14.7.3.2 'During': **rawàaŋ**

rawàaŋ dʉan meesǎa
ระหว่างเดือนเมษาฯ
during April

14.7.3.3 'Middle': **klaaŋ**

klaaŋ dʉan nâa
กลางเดือนหน้า
the middle of next month

14.7.3.4 'End': **sîn/plaay**

sîn/plaay pii níi
สิ้น/ปลายปีนี้
the end of this year

14.7.4 *'Ago', 'in . . . time', 'within', 'since'*

14.7.4.1 'Ago': (mûa) . . . kɔɔn/thîi lɛɛw/maa lɛɛw/maa níi

'Ago' is normally expressed using (mûa) + NUMBER + UNIT OF TIME +
either kɔɔn or thîi lɛɛw or maa lɛɛw or maa níi, which can be used
interchangeably. Note, however that 'a moment ago' is a set phrase which
does not follow this pattern.

(mûa) hâa pii kɔɔn
(เมื่อ)ห้าปีก่อน
five years ago

(mûa) cèt dʉan thîi lɛɛw
(เมื่อ)เจ็ดเดือนที่แล้ว
seven months ago

(mûa) sǎam wan maa lɛɛw
(เมื่อ)สามวันมาแล้ว
three days ago

(mûa) sɔ̌ɔŋ sǎam naathii maa níi
(เมื่อ)สองสามนาทีมานี้
two or three minutes ago

mûa kîi níi (eeŋ)/mûa takîi níi (eeŋ)
เมื่อกี้นี้(เอง)/เมื่อตะกี้นี้(เอง)
(just) a moment ago

14.7.4.2 'In . . . time': ìik

ìik hòk wan
อีกหกวัน
in six days' time

14.7.4.3 'Within': phaay nay

phaay nay sǎam dʉan
ภายในสามเดือน
within three months

14.7.4.4 'Since': tâŋtɛɛ

tâŋtɛɛ mûa waan
ตั้งแต่เมื่อวาน
since yesterday

14.7.5 Duration of time

Duration of time (I'm going *for* two weeks) is most commonly expressed by the pattern VERB (PHRASE) + EXPRESSION OF TIME; there is no preposition in Thai corresponding to English 'for':

phǒm pay sɔ̌ɔŋ aathít
ผมไปสองอาทิตย์
I'm going for two weeks.

kháw rian phaasǎa thay sǎam pii
เขาเรียนภาษาไทยสามปี
She studied Thai for 3 years.

Two alternative patterns for expressing duration of time are (a) VERB (PHRASE) + **pen weelaa** + EXPRESSION OF TIME; and (b) VERB (PHRASE) + **dâay** + EXPRESSION OF TIME; the latter is used only in the past continuous tense:

kháw ca rian pen weelaa sǎam pii
เขาจะเรียนเป็นเวลาสามปี
He will study for three years.

chán sɔ̌ɔn phaasǎa aŋkrìt (maa) dâay cèt dɯan lɛ́ɛw
ฉันสอนภาษาอังกฤษ(มา)ได้เจ็ดเดือนแล้ว
I have been teaching English for seven months.

14.8 Telling the time

14.8.1 Hours

Telling the time in Thai is complicated by the fact that the hour word, equivalent to 'o'clock' in English, varies according to the time of day and, with it, the position of the hour number:

tii + NUMBER	1 a.m.–5 a.m.
NUMBER + **mooŋ cháaw**	6 a.m.–11 a.m.
bàay + NUMBER + **mooŋ**	1 p.m.–4 p.m.
NUMBER + **mooŋ yen**	5 p.m.–6 p.m.
NUMBER + **thûm**	7 p.m.–11 p.m.

The hours from 6a.m. to 11a.m. can be counted using numbers 6–11 + **mooŋ cháaw**, or in an alternative way based on a division of the day in to six-hour periods, starting from 7 a.m., whereby 8 a.m. becomes '2 o'clock in the morning', 9 a.m. '3 o'clock . . .', and so on:

midnight	**thîaŋ khʉʉn**	เที่ยงคืน
1 a.m	**tii nʉ̀ŋ**	ตีหนึ่ง
2 a.m.	**tii sɔ̌ɔŋ**	ตีสอง
3 a.m.	**tii sǎam**	ตีสาม
4 a.m.	**tii sìi**	ตีสี่
5 a.m.	**tii hâa**	ตีห้า
6 a.m.	**hòk mooŋ cháaw**	หกโมงเช้า
7 a.m.	**cèt mooŋ cháaw**	เจ็ดโมงเช้า
or	**mooŋ cháaw**	โมงเช้า
8 a.m.	**pὲɛt mooŋ cháaw**	แปดโมงเช้า
or	**sɔ̌ɔŋ mooŋ cháaw**	สองโมงเช้า
9 a.m.	**kâaw mooŋ cháaw**	เก้าโมงเช้า
or	**sǎam mooŋ cháaw**	สามโมงเช้า
10 a.m.	**sìp mooŋ cháaw**	สิบโมงเช้า
or	**sìi mooŋ cháaw**	สี่โมงเช้า
11 a.m.	**sìp èt mooŋ cháaw**	สิบเอ็ดโมงเช้า
or	**hâa mooŋ cháaw**	ห้าโมงเช้า
midday	**thîaŋ (wan)**	เที่ยง(วัน)
1 p.m.	**bàay mooŋ**	บ่ายโมง
2 p.m.	**bàay sɔ̌ɔŋ mooŋ**	บ่ายสองโมง
3 p.m.	**bàay sǎam mooŋ**	บ่ายสามโมง
4 p.m.	**bàay sìi mooŋ**	บ่ายสี่โมง
5 p.m.	**hâa mooŋ yen**	ห้าโมงเย็น
6 p.m.	**hòk mooŋ yen**	หกโมงเย็น
7 p.m.	**thûm nʉ̀ŋ**	ทุ่มหนึ่ง
8 p.m.	**sɔ̌ɔŋ thûm**	สองทุ่ม

9 p.m.	**săam thûm**	สามทุ่ม
10 p.m.	**sìi thûm**	สี่ทุ่ม
11 p.m.	**hâa thûm**	ห้าทุ่ม

Note: **tii** and **bàay** appear before the number; **tii** and **thûm** do not occur with **moon**.

A traditional way of counting the hours of darkness, still used among elderly people in Bangkok and in rural areas, uses the word **yaam** ('a 3-hour watch period'):

9 p.m.	**yaam nùŋ**	ยามหนึ่ง
midnight	**sɔ̌ɔŋ yaam**	สองยาม
3 a.m.	**săam yaam**	สามยาม

14.8.2 Half-hours

Half-past the hour is expressed as HOUR TIME + **khrɨ̂ŋ** ('half'). For the hours from 7 a.m. to 11 a.m., however, the word **cháaw** is usually omitted:

3.30 a.m.	**tii săam khrɨ̂ŋ**	ตีสามครึ่ง
7.30 a.m.	**cèt moon khrɨ̂ŋ**	เจ็ดโมงครึ่ง
11.30 a.m.	**sìp èt moon khrɨ̂ŋ**	สิบเอ็ดโมงครึ่ง
2.30 p.m.	**bàay sɔ̌ɔŋ moon khrɨ̂ŋ**	บ่ายสองโมงครึ่ง
5.30 p.m.	**hâa moon yen khrɨ̂ŋ**	ห้าโมงเย็นครึ่ง
10.30 p.m.	**sìi thûm khrɨ̂ŋ**	สี่ทุ่มครึ่ง

14.8.3 Quarter hours and minutes past/to the hour

There is no special word for 'quarter past' or 'quarter to' the hour. Minutes past the hour are expressed as HOUR TIME + NUMBER + **naathii** ('minutes'):

10.15 a.m.	**sìp moon sìp hâa naathii**	สิบโมงสิบห้านาที
2.10 p.m.	**bàay sɔ̌ɔŋ moon sìp naathii**	บ่ายสองโมงสิบนาที
9.15 p.m.	**săam thûm sìp hâa naathii**	สามทุ่มสิบห้านาที

Minutes to the hour are expressed as **ìik** ('further, more') + NUMBER + **naathii** ('minutes') + HOUR TIME:

10.45 a.m.   **ìik sìp hâa naathii sìp èt mooŋ**
อีกสิบห้านาทีสิบเอ็ดโมง

5.40 p.m.   **ìik yîi sìp naathii hòk mooŋ yen**
อีกยี่สิบนาทีหกโมงเย็น

11.55 p.m.   **ìik hâa naathii thîaŋ khʉʉn**
อีกห้านาทีเที่ยงคืน

The 24-hour clock system

In the 24-hour clock system hours are expressed as NUMBER + **naalikaa** ('clock, o'clock'); half-hours are expressed as NUMBER + **naalikaa** + **sǎam sìp naathii** ('thirty minutes'):

16.00   **sìp hòk naalikaa**
สิบหกนาฬิกา

20.30   **yîi sìp naalikaa sǎam sìp naathii**
ยี่สิบนาฬิกาสามสิบนาที

Asking the time

To ask the time **kìi mooŋ?** or **weelaa thâwrày?** is used; to ask what time something happens or happened ... **kìi mooŋ?** is used:

kìi mooŋ lέεw?/weelaa thâwrày lέεw?
กี่โมงแล้ว/เวลาเท่าไรแล้ว
What time is it?

rót ɔ̀ɔk kìi mooŋ?
รถออกกี่โมง
What time does the bus leave?

Chapter 15

Thai speech conventions

15.1 Politeness

Politeness can be conveyed verbally in Thai by the appropriate choice of vocabulary, such as polite final particles (10.2), deferential pronouns (4.1) and formal vocabulary. As in most languages, the pitch and volume of voice can also be used to convey politeness. Speaking Thai softly and undemonstratively can be both a mark of politeness (reflecting the speaker's unwillingness to be too assertive) and a sign of authority and high status (reflecting the speaker's lack of need to be assertive); the foreigner who assumes these to be signs of weakness and indecision is likely to become culturally lost very quickly.

15.2 Thanks

The most widely used word for thank you is **khɔ̀ɔp khun**. When speaking to children or subordinates, **khɔ̀ɔp cay** may be used instead, and **khɔ̀ɔp phrakhun** when speaking to those of higher social status, or when wishing to be especially polite. All of these forms can be intensified by adding **mâak** ('much') or its reduplicated form **mâak mâak**:

khɔ̀ɔp khun (mâak) khráp/khâ
ขอบคุณ(มาก)ครับ/ค่ะ
Thank you (very much).

khɔ̀ɔp phrakhun
ขอบพระคุณ
Thank you (especially polite and to superiors).

khɔ̀ɔp cay
ขอบใจ
Thank you (to children and subordinates).

Thanking someone for doing something is expressed by the pattern **khɔ̀ɔp khun + thîi + VERB (PHRASE)**:

khɔ̀ɔp khun thîi bɔ̀ɔk lûaŋ nâa
ขอบคุณที่บอกล่วงหน้า
Thank you for telling me in advance.

Thanking someone for something is expressed by the pattern **khɔ̀ɔp khun + sǎmràp + NOUN (PHRASE)**:

khɔ̀ɔp khun sǎmràp thúk sìŋ thúk yàaŋ
ขอบคุณสำหรับทุกสิ่งทุกอย่าง
Thank you for everything.

Thanks can be acknowledged (a) silently, with a smile or a nod; (b) by **khráp** (male speakers) or **khâ** (female speakers); or (c) by **mây pen ray** ('never mind; that's alright; don't mention it'):

khɔ̀ɔp khun mâak khráp
ขอบคุณมากครับ
Thank you very much.

– mây pen ray khâ
– ไม่เป็นไรค่ะ
– That's alright.

15.3 Apologies

The essential word for apologising is **khɔ̌othôot**; in informal situations it is often shortened to **'thôot**. In more formal situations, **khɔ̌ɔ aphay** may be used, or even more formally, **khɔ̌ɔ prathaan thôot**. **khɔ̌othôot** can be intensified by **mâak mâak** or **ciŋ ciŋ**:

khɔ̌othôot khráp/khâ
ขอโทษครับ/ค่ะ
Sorry; please excuse me.

khɔ̌othôot mâak mâak/ciŋ ciŋ
ขอโทษมากๆ/จริงๆ
I'm ever so sorry.

khɔ̌ɔ aphay
ขออภัย
Sorry; please excuse me (formal).

khɔ̌ɔ prathaan thôot
ขอประทานโทษ
Sorry; please excuse me (very formal).

201

In everyday speech, khɔ̌ɔthôot is commonly followed by the mood particles thii or dûay ná (10.3); 'thôot thii is used to apologise for tiny errors,
while khɔ̌ɔthôot dûay ná conveys a stronger sense of apology:

(khɔ̌ɔ) thôot thii
(ขอ)โทษที
Sorry.

khɔ̌ɔthôot dûay ná
ขอโทษด้วยนะ
Sorry.

Apologising for doing something is expressed by the pattern khɔ̌ɔthôot
thii + VERB (PHRASE):

khɔ̌ɔthôot thîi rópkuan
ขอโทษที่รบกวน
Sorry for disturbing you.

Note that thîi here has a falling tone and is not to be confused with the
final particle thii in thôot thii.

The expression sǐa cay ('I'm sorry') is an expression of sympathy or regret
rather than an apology (15.6.3).

15.4 Polite requests

15.4.1 Requests for information

Basic requests for information can be prefaced by khɔ̌ɔthôot khráp/khâ
('excuse me') for politeness:

khɔ̌ɔthôot khráp/khâ, rót ɔ̀ɔk kìi mooŋ?
ขอโทษครับ/ค่ะ รถออกกี่โมง
Excuse me, what time does the train leave?

khɔ̌ɔthôot khráp/khâ, praysanii yùu thîi nǎy?
ขอโทษครับ/ค่ะ ไปรษณีย์อยู่ที่ไหน
Excuse me, where is the Post Office?

15.4.2 Requests for something

Requests for something are expressed by the pattern khɔ̌ɔ + NOUN
(PHRASE) + (dâay máy)?:

khɔ̌ɔ nám khɛ̌ŋ plàaw sɔ̌ɔŋ kɛ̂ɛw (dâay máy)?
ขอน้ำแข็งเปล่าสองแก้ว(ได้ไหม)
Could I have two glasses of water, please?

If the noun is unquantified (i.e. 'water' rather than 'two glasses of water'), then it is often followed by nɔ̀y ('a little') for politeness:

khɔ̌ɔ khâaw nɔ̀y (dâay máy)?
ขอข้าวหน่อย(ได้ไหม)
Could I have some rice, please?

... dâay máy? is an optional additional politeness expression.

15.4.3 | **Requests to do something oneself**

Requests to do something oneself can be expressed by the pattern **khɔ̌ɔ** + VERB (PHRASE) + **nɔ̀y** + (dâay máy)?:

khɔ̌ɔ duu nɔ̀y?
ขอดูหน่อย
Can I have a look, please?

khɔ̌ɔ phûut kàp khun tɔ̌y nɔ̀y dâay máy?
ขอพูดกับคุณต้อยหน่อยได้ไหม
Could I speak to Khun Toi, please?

15.4.4 | **Requesting someone to do something**

Requesting someone to do something for you or someone else is expressed by the pattern **chûay** + VERB (PHRASE):

chûay pìt pratuu
ช่วยปิดประตู
Please close the door.

chûay ... requests are often used with the mood particles **dûay ná** or **nɔ̀y** (10.3); ... **dâay máy?** ('could you ...?') can also be added at the end of the sentence for politeness:

chûay pìt pratuu dûay ná dâay máy?
ช่วยปิดประตูด้วยนะได้ไหม
Please could you close the door.

chûay pìt pratuu nɔ̀y dâay máy?
ช่วยปิดประตูหน่อยได้ไหม
Please could you close the door.

To indicate the beneficiary of the action (i.e. who it is being done for), the pattern may be expanded to **chûay** + VERB (PHRASE) + **hây** (+ BENE-FICIARY) (+ **nɔ̀y**):

chûay pìt thii wii hây
ช่วยปิดทีวีให้
Please turn the TV off (for me).

chûay plɛɛ hây kháw nɔ̀y
ช่วยแปลให้เขาหน่อย
Please translate for him.

chûay sàŋ aahǎan hây (phǒm) nɔ̀y
ช่วยสั่งอาหารให้(ผม)หน่อย
Please order food for me.

Two rather more formal words for requesting someone to do something are **karunaa** and **pròot**, both of which can be translated as 'please'; **karunaa** often follows **chûay** in very formal polite conversation, while **pròot** can be heard at the beginning of public announcements:

chûay karunaa bɔ̀ɔk kháw dûay
ช่วยกรุณาบอกเขาด้วย
Please tell him.

pròot sâap . . .
โปรดทราบ . . .
Please be informed that . . .

Both **karunaa** and **pròot** also occur commonly on public signs:

karunaa thɔ̀ɔt rɔɔŋ tháaw
กรุณาถอดรองเท้า
Please remove your shoes.

karunaa kòt kriŋ
กรุณากดกริ่ง
Please ring the bell.

pròot ŋîap
โปรดเงียบ
Please be quiet.

Requesting someone not to do something

The least confrontational way to ask someone not to do something is to use the expression **mây tôŋ . . .** ('there's no need to . . .'). More direct requests employ the negative imperative **yàa . . .** ('Don't . . .') (11.8) which can be 'softened' by the addition of the mood particle **ná** (10.3) or made more tactful, polite and deferential by prefixing the polite request words **chûay, karunaa** or, more formally, **pròot. hâam . . .** ('to forbid') is an unambiguous order rather than a request, commonly found on notices of prohibition (see also 11.9); in speech, it can be 'softened' by the addition of the particle **ná**:

mây tôŋ pìt pratuu ná
ไม่ต้องปิดประตูนะ
There's no need to shut the door.

chûay yàa pìt pratuu ná
ช่วยอย่าปิดประตูนะ
Please don't shut the door.

karunaa yàa pìt pratuu ná
กรุณาอย่าปิดประตูนะ
Please don't shut the door.

yàa pìt pratuu ná
อย่าปิดประตูนะ
Don't shut the door, OK?

hâam pìt pratuu ná
ห้ามปิดประตูนะ
Don't shut the door, OK!

hâam khâw
ห้ามเข้า
No Entry!

hâam sùup bùrìi
ห้ามสูบบุหรี่
No Smoking!

Inviting someone to do something

Inviting someone to do something, such as sit down, come in, start eating, is expressed by the pattern **chəən** ('to invite') + VERB (PHRASE). The mood article **sí** (10.3) is commonly added to **chəən** . . . invitations:

chəən nâŋ sí khráp/khá
เชิญนั่งซิครับ/คะ
Please sit down.

chəən khâaŋ nay sí khráp/khá
เชิญข้างในซิครับ/คะ
Please come in.

chəən sí khráp/khá
เชิญซิครับ/คะ
Carry on; go ahead; after you.

15.5 Misunderstandings

Expressing ignorance, uncertainty

Thai cannot use the same verb for knowing facts and knowing people or places; **rúu** (informal) or **sâap** (formal, deferential) mean 'to know facts' while **rúucàk** means 'to know or be acquainted with people, places or things':

chán mây rúu/sâap
ฉันไม่รู้/ทราบ
I don't know.

kháw mây rúucàk phǒm
เขาไม่รู้จักผม
He doesn't know me.

mây rúucàk kham wâa . . .
ไม่รู้จักคำว่า . . .
I don't know the word . . .

phǒm mây nɛ̂ɛ (cay)
ผมไม่แน่(ใจ)
I'm not sure.

15.5.2 *Expressing non-comprehension*

There are two words for 'to understand': **khâw cay** and **rúu rûaŋ**:

phǒm mây khâw cay
ผมไม่เข้าใจ
I don't understand.

kháw mây rúu rûaŋ
เขาไม่รู้เรื่อง
He doesn't understand.

rúu rûaŋ and **khâw cay** often occur as resultative verbs (5.4) with **faŋ** ('to listen') and **àan** ('to read') in questions like **faŋ rúu rûaŋ máy?** ('do you understand (what you hear)?') and **àan rúu rûaŋ máy?** ('do you understand (what you read)?'). In negative statements the word order is VERB (PHRASE) + **mây** + RESULTATIVE VERB (11.2):

kháw faŋ mây rúu rûaŋ
เขาฟังไม่รู้เรื่อง
He doesn't understand (what he hears).

chán àan mây rúu rûaŋ
ฉันอ่านไม่รู้เรื่อง
I don't understand (what I read).

than ('to catch up with', in time) is also used as a resultative verb with **faŋ** ('to listen') to express the idea that non-comprehension is due to the speaker speaking too quickly:

phǒm faŋ (khruu) mây than
ผมฟัง(ครู)ไม่ทัน
I don't understand (the teacher) (because he speaks too quickly).

15.5.3 *Asking someone to repeat, speak slowly, explain,
translate, spell*

aray ná khráp/khá
อะไรนะครับ/คะ
Pardon?

phûut ìik thii dâay máy?
พูดอีกทีได้ไหม
Could you say that again?

phûut cháa cháa nɔ̀y dâay máy?

พูดช้า ๆ หน่อยได้ไหม

Could you speak slowly, please?

There are two ways of asking what something means: **mǎay khwaam wâa aray?** is a request for clarification or an explanation, while **plɛɛ wâa aray?** seeks a translation:

. . . mǎay khwaam wâa aray?

. . . หมายความว่าอะไร

What does . . . mean?

. . . plɛɛ wâa aray?

. . . แปลว่าอะไร

What does . . . mean?

. . . phaasǎa aŋkrìt plɛɛ wâa aray?

. . . ภาษาอังกฤษแปลว่าอะไร

What is . . . in English?

phaasǎa aŋkrìt plɛɛ wâa aray?

ภาษาอังกฤษแปลว่าอะไร

What is it in English?

phaasǎa thay khǐan yaŋŋay?

ภาษาไทยเขียนอย่างไร

How is it written in Thai?

sakòt yaŋŋay?

สะกดอย่างไร

How do you spell it?

15.6　Socialising

Initial conversations between Thais and foreigners are likely to involve the exchange of personal information. Westerners tend to find some questions, like *Do you have any brothers and sisters?* , surprising and others, like *How much do you earn?* or *Why haven't you got any children yet?* irritating, intrusive or downright impolite, as in fact most Thais would. But these are easily outweighed, for most Westerners, by the Thais' capacity for saying nice things, such as *You speak Thai well!*, *That's a nice dress you're wearing!* or *You're looking handsome today!* Westerners, perhaps unused to a culture of mutual personal compliments, often make the mistake of taking compliments too literally and, even more often, do not even consider making a return compliment at the next opportune moment. Compliments can be accepted with a gracious **khɔ̀ɔp khun** ('thank you') or modestly denied **mây rɔ̀k khráp/khâ** ('not at all'):

khun phûut thay kèŋ/chát
คุณพูดไทยเก่ง/ชัด
You speak Thai well/clearly.

– mây rɔ̀k khráp/khâ
– ไม่หรอกครับ/ค่ะ
– Not at all.

Other typical compliments include:

tèŋ tua sǔay/lɔ̀ɔ
แต่งตัวสวย/หล่อ
You look nice (i.e. are nicely dressed)!

tham aahǎan arɔ̀y
ทำอาหารอร่อย
Your cooking tastes good.

| 15.6.1 | *Greetings, introductions, farewells* |

The basic greeting **sawàt dii**, often abbreviated to **'wàt dii** in speech, is used for both formal and informal greetings regardless of the time of day; it is often accompanied by a *wai*, a gesture in which the head is bowed slightly and the hands held in a prayer-like position, somewhere between neck and forehead height, depending on the status of the person being greeted. **sawàt dii** can also be used when taking leave.

More casual greetings are **pay nǎy?** ('Where are you going?') and **pay nǎy maa?** ('Where have you been?') which do not normally require a precise answer; in the workplace, **thaan khâaw rʉ́ yaŋ** ('Have you eaten yet?') is often more a midday greeting, than an invitation to lunch together:

sawàt dii khráp/khâ
สวัสดีครับ/ค่ะ
Hello, good morning/afternoon, etc.; goodbye

sabaay dii lɔ̌ə?/pen yaŋŋay bâaŋ?
สบายดีหรือ/เป็นอย่างไรบ้าง
How are you?

– sabaay dii/kɔ̂ rʉ̂ay rʉ̂ay
– สบายดี/ก็ เรื่อย ๆ
– Fine/Same as usual.

pay nǎy?

ไปไหน

Hello (casual). (lit. Where are you going?)

– **pay thîaw**

ไปเที่ยว

I'm going out.

– **pay thúrá**

ไปธุระ

I'm going on business.

– **mây pay nǎy**

ไม่ไปไหน

I'm not going anywhere.

pay nǎy maa?

ไปไหนมา

Hello (casual). (lit. Where have you been?)

– **pay thîaw maa**

ไปเที่ยวมา

I've been out.

– **pay thúrá maa**

ไปธุระมา

I've been on business.

– **mây dây pay nǎy**

ไม่ได้ไปไหน

I haven't been anywhere.

thaan khâaw rɨ́ yaŋ?

ทานข้าวหรือยัง

Hello (informal, polite). (lit. Have you eaten yet?)

– **thaan lɛ́ɛw/yaŋ khráp(khâ)**

– ทานแล้ว/ยังครับ(ค่ะ)

– Yes/No.

khɔ̌ɔ nɛ́nam hây rúucàk kàp . . .

ขอแนะนำให้รู้จักกับ . . .

I'd like to introduce you to . . .

yin dii thîi rúucàk

ยินดีที่รู้จัก

Pleased to meet you.

pay lá ná/pay kɔ̀ɔn

ไปละนะ/ไปก่อน

Goodbye; I'm off now.

The basic personal questions below can be prefaced by **khɔ̌ɔthôot khráp/ khâ** ('excuse me') as a sign of politeness.

chɯ̂ɯ aray?
ชื่ออะไร
What's your (first) name?

naam sakun aray?
นามสกุลอะไร
What's your surname?

pen khon châat aray?
เป็นคนชาติอะไร
What nationality are you?

maa càak nǎy?
มาจากไหน
Where do you come from?

thîi . . . troŋ nǎy?
ที่ . . . ตรงไหน
Whereabouts in . . .?

maa càak mɯaŋ/caŋwàt aray?
มาจากเมือง/จังหวัดอะไร
Which town/province do you come from?

tham ŋaan aray?
ทำงานอะไร
What (job) do you do?

tham ŋaan thîi nǎy?
ทำงานที่ไหน
Where do you work?

mii phîi nɔ́ɔŋ máy?
มีพี่น้องไหม
Have you got any brothers and sisters?

aayú thâwrày?
อายุเท่าไร
How old are you?

tὲŋ ŋaan rɨ yaŋ?
แต่งงานหรือยัง
Are you married?

mii khrɔ̂ɔpkhrua rɨ yaŋ?
มีครอบครัวหรือยัง
Are you married? (lit. Do you have a family?)

mii lûuk rɨ yaŋ?
มีลูกหรือยัง
Do you have any children?

15.6.3 Expressing congratulations, sympathy

Congratulations and sympathy can be expressed formally using the expresssion **khɔ̌ɔ sadɛɛŋ . . .** ('I would like to show . . .') which may be followed by the final particles **dûay ná** (10.3):

khɔ̌ɔ sadɛɛŋ khwaam yin dii (dûay ná)
ขอแสดงความยินดี(ด้วยนะ)
Congratulations!

khɔ̌ɔ sadɛɛŋ khwaam sǐa cay (dûay ná)
ขอแสดงความเสียใจ(ด้วยนะ)
I'd like to express my regret/sympathy.

15.6.4 Telephone transactions

The English word 'hello', pronounced in a more or less Thai way (**hanlǒo**), is used at the beginning of phone calls; the greeting/farewell **sawàt dii/ 'wàt dii** or, more informally, **khêɛ níi ná** ('That's all for now') can be used at the end of the call:

khɔ̌ɔ phûut kàp khun . . . nɔ̀y dâay máy?
ขอพูดกับคุณ . . . หน่อยได้ไหม
Could I speak to . . ., please?

khray phûut khráp/khá?
ใครพูดครับ/คะ
Who's speaking, please?

khun . . . chây máy khráp/khá?
คุณ . . . ใช่ไหมครับ/คะ
Is that . . .?

phǒm/chán . . . phûut khráp/khâ
ผม/ฉัน . . . พูดครับ/ค่ะ
This is . . . speaking.

(chûay) phûut daŋ daŋ nɔ̀y dâay máy?
(ช่วย)พูดดัง ๆ หน่อยได้ไหม
Could you speak up a little, please?

mây khɔ̀y dây yin
ไม่ค่อยได้ยิน
I can scarcely hear.

rɔɔ sàk khrûu khráp/khâ
รอสักครู่ครับ/ค่ะ
Hold on a moment, please.

sǎay mây dii
สายไม่ดี
The line's bad.

sǎay mây wâaŋ
สายไม่ว่าง
The line isn't free.

sǎay lùt
สายหลุด
I got cut off.

khɔ̌ɔ tɔ̀ɔ bəə . . . ?
ขอต่อเบอร์ . . .
Could I have extension . . ., please?

ca sàŋ aray máy?
จะสั่งอะไรไหม
Do (you) want to leave a message?

chûay bɔ̀ɔk khun tĭm wâa . . .
ช่วยบอกคุณติ๋มว่า . . .
Please tell Khun Tim that . . .

chûay bɔ̀ɔk khun tĭm hây thoo thɯ̌ŋ chán dûay ná
ช่วยบอกคุณติ๋มให้โทรถึงฉันด้วยนะ
Please tell Khun Tim to ring me back.

khɛ̂ɛ níi ná
แค่นี้นะ
That's all for now.

lέεw ca thoo maa mày

แล้ว จะโทรมาใหม่

I'll ring back later.

yen yen ca thoo maa mày

เย็นๆ จะโทรมาใหม่

I'll ring back this evening.

khɔ̌ɔthôot thoo phìt bəə

ขอโทษ โทรผิดเบอร์

Sorry, I've got the wrong number.

Romanisation systems

There are many different ways of Romanising Thai. The system used throughout this book is based on one devised by the American linguist, Mary Haas. This system is widely used in university departments where Thai is taught and in the linguistic literature on Thai. As well as learning unfamiliar symbols from the International Phonetic Alphabet, such as ə, ɛ, ʉ, etc., the learner also has to recognise that ph and th are not pronounced like the initial consonant sound in 'phobia' and 'thin'. To avoid such problems, some materials (e.g. *Teach Yourself Thai, Robertson's Practical English-Thai Dictionary*) use non-technical systems of Romanisation, attempting to represent unfamiliar Thai sounds with combinations of letters such as '-air-o', 'dt' and 'eu-a'. Librarians and historians generally prefer the Library of Congress system, which, unlike systems used in language-learning, does not attempt to represent tone.

This is how an article entitled 'The turning point in Thai literature' would be Romanised according to three different systems:

หัวเลี้ยวของวรรณคดีไทย

Essential Grammar (EG)	**hǔa líaw khɔ̌ɔŋ wannakhadii thay**
Teach Yourself Thai (TYT)	**hǒo-a lée-o kǒrng wun-na-ka-dee tai**
Library of Congress (LC)	**hūa līeo khǫng wannakhadī thai**

	Essential Grammar		Teach Yourself Thai		Library of Congress	
	initial	final	initial	final	initial	final
CONSONANTS						
ก	k	k	g	k	k	k
ข	kh	k	k	k	kh	k
ค	kh	k	k	k	kh	k
ฆ	kh	k	k	k	kh	k
ง	ŋ	ŋ	ng	ng	ng	ng
จ	c	t	j	t	čh	t
ฉ	ch	t	ch	t	ch	t
ช	ch	t	ch	t	ch	t
ซ	s	t	s	t	s	t
ฌ	ch	t	ch	t	ch	t
ญ	y	n	y	n	y	n
ฎ	d	t	d	t	d	t
ฏ	t	t	dt	t	t	t
ฐ	th	t	t	t	th	t
ฑ	th	t	t	t	th	t
ฒ	th	t	t	t	th	t
ณ	n	n	n	n	n	n
ด	d	t	d	t	d	t
ต	t	t	dt	t	t	t
ถ	th	t	t	t	th	t
ท	th	t	t	t	th	t
ธ	th	t	t	t	th	t
น	n	n	n	n	n	n
บ	b	p	b	p	b	p
ป	p	p	bp	p	b	p
ผ	ph	p	p	p	ph	p
ฝ	f	p	f	p	f	p
พ	ph	p	p	p	ph	p

Appendix section, page 217.

Thai	EG	LC	EG	LC	EG	LC
ฟ	f	p	f	p	f	p
ภ	ph	p	p	p	ph	p
ม	m	m	m	m	m	m
ย	y	y	y	y	y	y
ร	r	n	r	n	r	n
ล	l	n	l	n	l	n
ว	w	w	w	w	w	w
ศ	s	t	s	t	s	t
ษ	s	t	s	t	s	t
ส	s	t	s	t	s	t
ห	h	—	h	—	h	—
ฬ	l	n	l	n	l	n
อ	—	—	—	—	—	—
ฮ	h	—	h	—	h	—

VOWELS

	EG	TYT	LC		EG	TYT	LC
-อ	-ɔɔ	-or	-ǭ	เ-อะ	-ə	-er	-œ
-ะ	-a	-a	-a	เ-ะ	-e	-e	-e
-ั	-a-	-u-	-a	เา	-aw	-ao	-ao
-ัว	-ua	-oo-a	-ūa	เ-าะ	-ɔ	-or	-ǫ
-า	-aa	-ah	-ā	เ-	-əə	-er	-ǭ̈
-ำ	-am	-um	-am	เ-ีย	-ia	-ee-a	-īa
-ิ	-i	-i	-i	เ-ียะ	-ia	-ee-a	-ia
-ี	-ii	-ee	-ī	เ-ือ	-ʉa	-eu-a	-ū'a
-ึ	-ʉ	-eu	-u'	แ-	-ɛɛ	-air	-ǣ
-ื	-ʉʉ	-eu	-ū'	แ-็	-ɛ	-air	-æ
-ุ	-u	-OO	-u	แ-ะ	-ɛ	-air	-æ
-ู	-uu	-oo	-ū	โ-	-oo	-oh	-ō
เ-	-ee	-ay	-ē	โ-ะ	-o	-o	-o
เ-็	-e	-e	-e	ใ-	-ay	-ai	-ai
เ-ย	əəy	-er-ee	-ǭ̈i	ไ-	-ay	-ai	-ai
เ-อ	-əə	-er	-ǭ̈				

Appendix 2

The verbs hây, dây/dâay and pen: a summary

The verbs, **hây**, **dây/dâay** and **pen** often seem confusing to the learner because each has several quite different meanings. This section summarises and cross-references the main patterns in which they are likely to be encountered.

1   *hây*

(a) SUBJECT + **hây** + DIRECT OBJECT + INDIRECT OBJECT (5.12)

As a main verb, **hây** means 'to give':

kháw hây ŋən chán
เขาให้เงินฉัน
He gave me money.

(b) SUBJECT + **hây** + INDIRECT OBJECT + VERB (PHRASE) (5.11)

As a causative verb, **hây** means 'to let (someone do something)' or 'to have (someone do something)':

kháw hây chán klàp bâan
เขาให้ฉันกลับบ้าน
He let me/had me go home.

(c) SUBJECT + VERB + **hây** + OBJECT + VERB (PHRASE) (5.11)

The manner of causation (e.g. telling, wanting, permitting someone to do something) can be specified by an appropriate verb preceding **hây**:

chán yàak hây khun chûay nɔ̀y
ฉันอยากให้คุณช่วยหน่อย
I'd like you to help me a bit.

218

Appendix 2
The verbs
hây, dây/dâay
and pen: a
summary

(d) SUBJECT + **tham** + **hây** + OBJECT + VERB (PHRASE) (5.11)

This pattern conveys a sense of intention or coercion on the part of the subject:

rûaŋ bɛ̀ɛp níi tham hây phǒm ramkhaan samǒǝ
เรื่องแบบนี้ทำให้ผมรำคาญเสมอ
This kind of thing always makes me annoyed.

(e) SUBJECT + VERB (PHRASE) + **hây** + INDIRECT OBJECT (8.3)

To convey the idea that the action is being carried out for the benefit of someone:

phǒm súɯ hây khun
ผมซื้อให้คุณ
I bought it for you.

(f) VERB (PHRASE) + **hây** + ADJECTIVE (7.1.5; 9.4)

As an adverb-marker in imperatives:

phûut hây chát nɔ̀y
พูดให้ชัดหน่อย
Speak clearly, please!

2 *dây/dâay*

Note that **dây** and **dâay** are spelt identically but the pronunciation varies according to its position in the sentence.

(a) **dây** + NOUN

As a main verb **dây** means 'to get':

khun dây ŋǝn dɯan thâwrày?
คุณได้เงินเดือนเท่าไร
How much salary do you get?

Appendix 2
The verbs
hây, dâ

y/dâay
and pen: a
summary

(b) **dây** + VERB (PHRASE)

As an auxiliary verb *before* the main verb, **dây** means 'to get to do something':

chán ca dây pay thîaw laaw
ฉันจะได้ไปเที่ยวลาว
I'll get to visit Laos.

(c) VERB (PHRASE) + **dâay** (5.6.2)

As an auxiliary verb *after* a verb or verb phrase, **dâay** means 'can, able to':

raw pay phrûŋ níi mây dâay
เราไปพรุ่งนี้ไม่ได้
We can't go tomorrow.

(d) VERB (PHRASE) + **dâay** + ADJECTIVE (7.1.4)

As an adverb-marker *after* the verb or verb phrase and before an adjective:

kháw phûut thay dâay dii
เขาพูดไทยได้ดี
He speaks Thai well.

(e) **mây dây** + VERB (PHRASE)

To indicate negative past (5.7.7):

raw mây dây pay
เราไม่ได้ไป
We didn't go.

or to contradict or correct a preceding statement or assumption (11.4):

kháw mây dây pen khon aŋkrit
เขาไม่ได้เป็นคนอังกฤษ
He's not English.

(f) INDEFINITE PRONOUN + **kɔ̂ dâay** (4.8.7); VERB
     (PHRASE)/NOUN + **kɔ̂ dâay**

To show amenability, a lack of preference or indifference:

khun pay mɯ̂arày kɔ̂ dâay
คุณไปเมื่อไรก็ได้
You can go whenever you like.

wan níi kɔ̂ dâay phrûŋ níi kɔ̂ dâay
วันนี้ก็ได้ พรุ่งนี้ก็ได้
Today is OK, tomorrow is OK.

pay kɔ̂ dâay mây pay kɔ̂ dâay
ไปก็ได้ ไมไปก็ได้
Going is fine by me, not going is fine, too.

Appendix 2
The verbs
hây, dây/dâay
and pen: a
summary

(g) VERB (PHRASE) + **(maa)** + **dâay** + TIME EXPRESSION (14.7.5)

To express duration of time (for . . .) for actions that began in the past and continue through to the present (5.7.8):

chán tham ŋaan thîi kruŋthêep (maa) dâay lǎay pii lɛ́ɛw
ฉันทำงานที่กรุงเทพฯ(มา)ได้หลายปีแล้ว
I have been working in Bangkok for several years.

3   *pen*

(a) **pen** + NOUN (5.1.1)

As the verb 'to be', it cannot normally be followed by an adjective (5.2); the negative is either **mây chây** + NOUN, or **mây dây pen** + NOUN:

kháw pen phɯ̂an
เขาเป็นเพื่อน
He's a friend.

(b) VERB (PHRASE) + **pen** (5.6.2)

As an auxiliary post-verb, meaning 'to know how to do something':

kháw wâay náam pen
เขาว่ายน้ำเป็น
He can swim.

(c) VERB (PHRASE) + **pen** + NOUN (PHRASE) (7.1.3)

As an adverb-marker:

kháw càay pen ŋən sòt
เขาจ่ายเป็นเงินสด
They paid in cash.

Appendix 2
The verbs
hây, dâay/dâay
and pen: a
summary

(d) VERB (PHRASE) + **pen** + EXPRESSION OF TIME (14.7.5)

To express duration of time:

kháw yùu thîi nîi pen weelaa naan
เขาอยู่ที่นี่เป็นเวลานาน
He's been here a long time.

(e) **pen** + DISEASE

Where English uses 'to have' or 'to get' with diseases and illnesses, Thai
uses **pen**:

khun pen wàt châap máy?
คุณเป็นหวัดใช่ไหม
You've got a cold, haven't you?

Glossary

Adjectives in Thai occur after the nouns they describe; they do not occur with the verb 'to be'. Adjectives also function as **stative verbs**; thus, **dii** is both the adjective 'good' and the stative verb 'to be good'. Adjectives and adverbs often take the same form in Thai; thus **dii** is both the adjective 'good' and the adverb 'well'.

Adverbs often occur after verbs. They can describe an action, where they often take the same form as **adjectives,** or the whole sentence.

Aspect is concerned with whether the action of a verb is complete, ongoing or habitual; it is marked in Thai by **auxiliary verbs.**

Auxiliary verbs only occur with other verbs; Thai auxiliaries include **modal** verbs and time and **aspect** markers.

Causative verbs in Thai convey a range of meanings including allowing something to happen, causing something to happen, either intentionally or unintentionally, and compelling someone to do something.

Classifiers are attributed to every noun and are used primarily, but not exclusively, in noun phrases involving numbers, such as 'three daughters', 'four glasses of orange juice', and so on.

Compounds are combinations of two words to make a new word. Compounding is an important derivational process in Thai in creating nouns, adjectives and verbs.

Concessive clauses concede a point which is then often countered in the following clause. In English they usually begin with 'although'; in Thai, the following clause is usually introduced by 'but'.

Conditional clauses commonly begin with 'if' and state a condition under which the following clause holds true. In Thai the 'if' word is often omitted.

Consonant class Thai consonants are divided into three classes – low, mid and high; the class of the initial consonant in a syllable will play a part in determining the tone of the syllable.

Consonant clusters are combinations of two consonant sounds, such as pl-, khw-, pr-; in Thai they occur only at the beginning of a syllable. The class of the first consonant in the cluster plays a part in determining the tone of the syllable.

Dead syllables are one of two types of syllable in Thai (see also **live syllables**); dead syllables are those which end in either in a **p, t** or **k** stop consonant or a short vowel.

Demonstratives are words like 'this' and 'that'. Thai demonstrative pronouns and demonstrative adjectives are distinguished by tone, pronouns having a falling tone and adjectives a high tone.

Diphthongs are glides from one 'pure' vowel sound to another.

Directional verbs occur after a verb (phrase) to indicate the direction of the action in relation to the speaker.

Intensifiers modify adjectives and adverbs expressing the degree to which that quality is present (e.g. very, fairly, hardly); many adjectives in Thai take their own specific intensifier (cf. *pitch* black).

Live syllables are one of two types of syllable in Thai (see also **dead syllables**); live syllables are those which end in either an **m, n, ŋ, w,** or **y** sound or a long vowel.

Modal verbs express possibility, probability, ability, necessity, volition and obligation. Most, but not all, Thai modals occur before a verb (phrase); modals are not all negated in the same way.

Noun phrases consist of a noun modified by one or more modifying words, such as numbers, demonstratives or adjectives. **Classifiers** play an important role in noun phrases in Thai.

Personal pronouns Thai has a much more complex system of personal pronouns than English; choice of the appropriate pronoun is determined not only by gender and number, but also by age, social status, context and personality; kin terms, status/occupation terms, personal names and nicknames are commonly used as pronouns; pronouns are also commonly omitted.

Quantifiers are words like 'all', 'some', 'many' and 'every'. In Thai noun phrases some quantifiers behave like numbers and others like adjectives.

Reduplication, most commonly involving the repetition of an adjective or an adverb, can serve a number of functions, including making the meaning less precise, intensifying the meaning and signalling an imperative; a small number of nouns can be pluralised by reduplication.

Resultative verbs occur after another verb to describe the state that results from the action of the first verb (cf. I shot him *dead*).

Sentence particles occur at the end of an utterance. They include question particles, which serve a grammatical function, and polite particles, mood particles and exclamatory particles, which have a communicative function.

Stative verbs describe a state rather than an action. Adjectives in Thai also function as stative verbs.

Subordinate clauses are dependent on the main clause in a sentence. They include concessive, conditional, purpose, reason and relative clauses.

Tone The pitch assigned to each syllable. Standard Thai has five tones – mid, high, low, rising and falling.

Topicalization involves placing a word or phrase other than the subject at the beginning of the sentence in order to highlight it and make it the 'topic' of the sentence.

Unreleased consonants occur when the airstream is closed to make the sound, but not re-opened; the final 'p' in English 'yep!' is commonly pronounced as an unreleased consonant. The final stop consonants in Thai (**p, t, k**) are unreleased.

Verb phrase This consists of a verb and optionally, its objects (direct and indirect) and any modifying adverb. In this book, the convention VERB (PHRASE) is used extensively to mean 'verb or verb phrase'.

Verb serialization is an extremely common feature of Thai in which a number of verbs sharing the same subject follow one another with no intervening conjunctions or prepositions.

Wh- questions are questions which begin with wh- in English: who?, whose?, what?, which?, where?, when?, why? How? is also normally included in this category.

Bibliography and further reading

Abramson, A.S. (ed.) (1997) *Southeast Asian Linguistic Studies in Honour of Vichin Panupong*, Bangkok: Chulalongkorn University Press.

Angkab Palakornkul (1972) 'A socio-linguistic study of pronominal strategy in spoken Bangkok Thai', unpublished PhD diss. University of Texas, Austin.

Anthony, E.M. *et al.* (1967, 1970) *Foundations of Thai*, 2 vols, Ann Arbor, MI: University of Michigan Press; Washington, DC: US Office of Education.

Brown, J.M. (1967–69) *AUA Language Center Thai Course*, 3 vols, Bangkok: American University Alumni Language Center.

—— (1979) *AUA Language Center Thai Course: Reading and Writing*, 2 vols, Bangkok: American University Alumni Language Center.

Campbell, R.N. (1969) *Noun Substitutes in Modern Thai: A Study in Pronominality*, Mouton: The Hague.

Campbell, S. and Chuan Shaweewongse (1957) *Fundamentals of the Thai Language*, Bangkok: S Bunyasiribhandu.

Chamberlain, J.R. (ed.) (1991) *The Ram Khamhaeng Controversy: Collected Papers*, Bangkok: Siam Society.

Cooke, J.R. (1968) *Pronominal Reference in Thai, Burmese and Vietnamese*, Berkeley and Los Angeles: University of California Press.

—— (1989) *Thai Sentence Particles and Other Topics*, Canberra: Australian National University.

Delouche, G. (1991) *Méthode de Thaï*, 2 vols Paris: L'Asiathèque.

Diller, A. (1985) 'High and low Thai: views from within', in D. Bradley (ed.) *Language Policy, Language Planning and Sociolinguistics in South-East Asia*, Canberra: Australian National University.

—— (1991) 'What makes Central Thai a National Language?', in C.J. Reynolds (ed.) *National Identity and Its Defenders: Thailand, 1939–1989*, Victoria, Australia: Monash University, Centre of Southeast Asian Studies.

Domnern Garden and Sathienpong Wannapok (1994) *Thai–English Dictionary*, Bangkok: Amarin Printing and Publishing pcl.

Gething, T.W., Harris, J.G. and Pranee Kullavanijaya (eds) (1976) *Tai Linguistics in Honor of Fang-Kuei Li*, Bangkok: Chulalongkorn University Press.

Haas, M. (1964) *Thai–English Student's Dictionary*, Stanford, CA: Stanford University Press.

Haas, M. and Heng R. Subhanka (1945–48) *Spoken Thai*, New York: Henry Holt.

Harris, J.G. and Chamberlain, J.R. (eds) (1975) *Studies in Tai Linguistics in Honor of William J. Gedney*, Bangkok: Central Institute of English Language, Office of State Universities.

Huffman, F.E. (1986) *Bibliography and Index of Mainland Southeast Asian Languages and Linguistics*, New Haven and London: Yale University Press.

Kuo, W. (1982) *Teaching Grammar of Thai,* Berkeley, CA: Centre for South and Southeast Asia Studies.

McFarland, G. B. (1944) *Thai-English Dictionary*, Stanford, CA: Stanford University Press.

Manas Chitakasem and Smyth, D.A. (1984) *Linguaphone Thai Course*, London: Linguaphone Institute.

Noss, R. (1964) *Thai Reference Grammar*, Washington, DC: Foreign Service Institute.

Palmer, A. (1974) *Small Talk*, Bangkok: American University Alumni Language Center.

—— (1977) *Getting Help with Your Thai*, Bangkok: American University Alumni Language Center.

Robertson, R. (1969) *Robertson's Practical English-Thai Dictionary*, Rutland, Vermont and Tokyo: Charles E. Tuttle.

Ru'angdet Pankhu'ankhat (1997) *Phasasat phasa thay* (Thai Linguistics), Salaya, Nakhorn Pathom: Mahidol University, Institute of Language and Culture for Rural Development.

Smalley, W.A. (1994) *Linguistic Diversity and National Unity*: *Language Ecology in Thailand*, Chicago and London: University of Chicago Press.

Smyth, D.A. (1995) *Teach Yourself Thai*, London: Hodder and Stoughton.

Thianchai Iamwaramet (1993) *A New Thai Dictionary with Bilingual Explanation*, Bangkok: Ruam San.

Vichin Panupong (1970) *Inter-sentence Relations in Modern Conversational Thai*, Bangkok: The Siam Society.

Voravudhi Chirasombutti and Diller, A. (1999) 'Who am "I" in Thai? – The Thai first person: self-reference or gendered self?', in P.A. Jackson and N.M. Cook (eds) *Genders and Sexualities in Modern Thailand*, Chiang Mai: Silkworm Books.

Yates, W. and Absorn Tryon (1970) *Thai Basic Course*, 2 vols, Washington, DC: Foreign Service Institute.

Index